Child Mining in an Era of High-Technology

Understanding the Roots, Conditions,
and Effects of Labor Exploitation in the
Democratic Republic of Congo

Roger-Claude Liwanga

Alpha Academic Press   Dearborn, Michigan

COPYRIGHT DISCLAIMER

Copyright © 2017 Roger-Claude Liwanga
First Edition, Paperback
Publication Date: March 2017
ISBN: 978-0-9975603-3-6

Liwanga, Roger-Claude

Child Mining in an Era of High-Technology:
Understanding the Roots, Conditions,
and Effects of Labor Exploitation in the
Democratic Republic of Congo

Alpha Academic Press
Published in the
United States of America

TABLE OF CONTENTS

LIST OF TABLES, FIGURES AND PHOTOGRAPHS

PREFACE

In 2013, I was flying back to Boston after my second field research on child labor trafficking in the mining industry in my native country of the Democratic Republic of Congo (DRC). I had only one thought in mind: to make a documentary highlighting the challenges and working conditions of child miners who I had met in the mines of eastern Congo. With no skills in filmmaking to edit the hours of footage and pictures that I had taken, I requested assistance from my colleagues at Harvard and Boston University. After many months, I finally had a twelve-minute documentary on child mining labor in the DRC. I wanted to launch that documentary by airing it on TV or posting it on YouTube so that everyone could know about this problem and, more important, understand the link between the minerals harvested by these children and the electronic devices that we use daily. It was aired once on WCVB/ABC-TV in Boston and screened at conferences at both Harvard and Boston Universities, but I quickly realized that posting the documentary on social media would twice victimize the child miners who appeared in it. I was concerned that child exploiters in the DRC, who have access to the internet, might watch the documentary and retaliate against the child miners who appeared in it. It then occurred to me that I should write a book where I could still tell a powerful story, but not put those children at risk. My goal was to provide a narrative that would expose the problem of child labor in the mining sector in the DRC.

Child labor exploitation is not a myth; it is a reality. According to the International Labor Organization (ILO), there were about 162 million child laborers in the world in 2012,[1] more than half of whom worked in hazardous industries such as mining.[2] In the DRC, the prevalence of child mining labor is high.[3] Although there is no official statistic on the number of child laborers in the country, at the time of writing this book it is estimated that children represent about 40% of the laborers in the DRC's artisanal mines.[4] There will likely be a higher percentage of child miners working in the mines by the time you read this book. Some child miners in the DRC work with family members or for themselves; others are recruited and supplied with tools by mine traders to extract various types of minerals. These children work more than ten hours a day to dig up, clean or sift ores that are used to produce the electronic devices that people cherish in the developed countries and regions, including the United States, Europe, Canada, and Japan. For example, cobalt is one of the raw ores produced by child miners in the DRC, and it is a fundamental component for rechargeable batteries in smart phones, tablets, and hybrid electric cars because of its capacity to hold a high electric charge.[5] By my calculation, at least 7.5% of the world's cobalt ores are extracted, transported, sifted or washed by children in the DRC.[6]

Children execute multiple tasks under inhumane conditions in the artisanal mines. These mines are considered artisanal because the mining exploitation is conducted through using manual and rudimentary methods to extract and process mined minerals.

Child miners use picks and shovels to dig minerals and heavy metal tools to crush ores. They transport loads of minerals on their heads from the mines to the rivers to wash them. These working conditions expose children to the risks of injuries, sicknesses and fatal accidents. In an open-pit mine in the DRC's province of Katanga, I met a child miner who walked with a limp because a big stone had fallen on his right leg and broken it while he was extracting minerals. I also spoke with a woman whose thirteen-year-old son was engulfed underground and killed while digging for cobalt ores. It was heartbreaking to hear these stories from child victims or their relatives. I was particularly sickened because some of these child victims were forced to continue working despite their injuries to earn just between $0.75 and $3.00 per day. When I tried to estimate the profit made those exploiting these children or those sourcing minerals directly or indirectly from them, I was filled with rage.

In January 2014, during the airing of my short documentary *Children of the Mines* on Boston's WCVB-TV, the *CityLine* host asked me how I first became involved in the issue of child mining labor. The origin of my research on this topic dates back years ago when I was working as a legal consultant at the Carter Center's Human Rights Program in Atlanta, Georgia. My first assignment was to review the pedagogical framework of a human rights training module for magistrates and police in the DRC. After completing that assignment, I was asked if I could be part of a legal team to develop another training module for Congolese judges and prosecutors on the prosecution of cases of child labor trafficking in the artisanal mines. I was hesitant to respond because it was the first time I had heard about child labor trafficking and its occurrence in the DRC's mining sector. I remember thinking to myself, how could I be a Congolese human rights lawyer and not know about child labor trafficking in the DRC's mines and, moreover, only learn about it in America. I thought that it couldn't possibly be true. I began reading reports, articles, and legal texts on human trafficking in the world, and particularly in the DRC. After doing my own research, I was shocked and ashamed. I was shocked by the story of a thirteen-year-old boy who was forced to drop out of school and work in the mines, and who was killed while digging for ores in a narrow and deep mining hole. And I was also ashamed of myself because of my ignorance of child exploitation occurring in "my own house." I finally agreed to be part of the team designing an anti-child trafficking training module and to do what I could to facilitate the prosecution of those exploiting and benefiting from child labor trafficking.

In spring 2011, I flew from Atlanta to the DRC's rich mining province of Katanga. Katanga is located in the southeastern part of the country and is as big as the combined size of the US states of California and West Virginia. When you read this book, Katanga will probably have been dismantled into four sub-provinces, as the DRC authorities are implementing an administrative decentralization program for some regions.[7] Yet, this province is particularly renowned because the United States used uranium ores from Katanga's Shinkolobwe mine to construct the first atomic bomb during World War II. Together with child protection experts from the Carter Center's Katanga field office, I organized a preliminary discussion with prosecutors, judges, and lawyers on protecting children from labor trafficking in the mining industry. The discussion was held at the Lubumbashi Bar Association (Lubumbashi is the capital city of Katanga), and I noted that the prosecutors and judges in Katanga knew of cases of child labor in the mines but that they lacked sufficient training and the means to investigate and prosecute child labor offenders.

During the spring 2011 trip, I did not have the opportunity to visit many mining sites, particularly the remote artisanal mining sites where a large population of children were reportedly working. I returned to Atlanta disappointed that I could not accomplish more or observe with own eyes what really happens in most of the artisanal mines. I stayed involved, conducting more desk research on child labor trafficking and thinking about a different approach to addressing this scourge. But I wanted to go back into the field to get first-hand testimony from child victims of labor exploitation.

It was nearly a year before I was able to return to the DRC. In April 2012 I went to Goma, a city in the North Kivu province of eastern Congo, to run training sessions on sexual and gender-based violent crimes for the American Bar Association Rule of Law Initiative (ABA-ROLI)'s staff. I planned to stay after my work was completed, hoping to use the opportunity to visit mining sites around North Kivu. I made arrangements with a guide and driver but could not move forward with my plans. There had been a panic the very same day that I landed in Goma's airport because a group of soldiers had mutinied and declared war against the local authorities. Owing to the situation, I did not attempt to visit the mining zones so as to avoid putting my life and those of my guides in danger.

I was determined to return to Katanga, however, and eight months later, in January 2013, I was able to go back. I rented a jeep, hired a driver and guide, and traveled hundreds of miles on unpaved and muddy roads to reach the remotest mining areas, sometimes driving during the night or walking on foot to get to places unreachable by car.

I visited as many remote mining sites as I could, more than ten in two districts, and conducted more than sixty interviews with children working in the artisanal mines. I also conducted interviews of the parents of child miners, mine traders, law enforcement officers, government officials, school authorities, and doctors and staff of NGOs. I sometimes posed as a mine trader in the mine trading houses (*comptoirs d'achat*) to observe who sourced minerals from children and what kind of parallel tasks children performed in the trading houses. The interviews with child miners or other informants ranged from thirty minutes to one hour. I conducted most of them in both French and Swahili language. I often used the service of an interpreter when the interviewees were more comfortable speaking in Swahili, as my fluency in that language is limited. My interviewees received no monetary compensation in exchange for talking to me.

Some of my interviews with child miners were conducted in the mining sites. My guide, who used to work as an artisanal miner, helped me to identify child miners who were willing to talk. In other places, I conducted interviews with child miners outside of the mining sites because I feared that the interviewees might be subject to reprisals after talking with me.

Most of my interviews with child miners were not videotaped. I felt more comfortable videotaping interviews with child miners who worked alongside their parents or other relatives. When interviews were recorded or videotaped, I carefully explained to each participant the consent form to be signed. However, while infrequent, there were times when I filmed activities inside the mine depots without the consent of the child miners or their employers. These cases arose when it was clear that I would not be able to expose or evidence the bad working conditions of children "employed" by the mine depots and trading houses if I openly disclosed my intentions. Indeed, interviewing child miners working for the mine depots and trading houses was almost an impossible mission because owners would hide the children from inspectors. One day, I posed as a furious mine trader and pretended that a group of child miners, who were working for me, had stolen my raw minerals and were hiding in a city where many trading houses were located. My trick worked. Using that cover, I was able to visit most of the mine depots and trade houses in the city of Musompo. I discovered that some mine depots have back rooms where children sift and wash minerals. From the outside, no one can see the children. But the children that I saw in one of the depots were cleaning loads of mined minerals in a big tank filled with water in a tiny, windowless room. The water was dirty and probably toxic, and the children were bent over and working without gloves or masks for protection. Their faces dripped with sweat as they worked. I could not talk to them because the depot's owners were always standing nearby.

Commonly, owners of mine lands, depots, and trading houses don't like "outsiders" to take pictures or try to speak with their child employees. One morning in 2013, on my way to Kolwezi to conduct more interviews, I arrived in Lwambo, where I saw a group of about ten girls and boys washing and lifting heavy loads of minerals. I asked the driver to stop the jeep because it was a bit surprising to see children working in an artisanal mine located just next to an asphalt main road. The driver stopped, and I took out my camera to film and take pictures of the mining activities from the jeep. Less than a minute later, men were running towards me from across the road. One of them held a big gun while another was on the phone. I asked the driver to get us away, but he told me that if we tried to run they would shoot at the car and follow us. So we stayed put. The man holding the gun stood in front of the car and pointed the gun at me. He threatened to shoot me if I didn't delete the footage and pictures I had taken. While I was deleting footage, I realized that another group of soldiers had also arrived at the scene. I saw that we had made a good decision to stay rather than run away because the situation could have gotten completely out of control. My guide, who was more fluent in Swahili than me, politely explained to those soldiers that I was not a journalist but only a curious person who wished to take pictures of the mine. Fortunately, they understood and let us go. Before leaving, I asked my guide to inquire why no pictures or footage could be taken of that mine. A soldier informed us that the mine belonged to the President's mother, and that they had been assigned to protect the mine--including from filming or picture-taking. Later, some NGO workers that I interviewed confirmed that certain government or parliamentary officials and their relatives own mines in the region. These officials either hire private security groups or assign soldiers or police officers to protect their properties. Thus, it is likely that the soldier was right. Later that evening, while I was alone in my hotel room, I was going through my photos and was surprised to find a short video clip of that mine that had escaped deletion, which I subsequently used in my documentary.

Of course, being a Congolese and being labeled as a (former) legal expert of an international NGO enabled me to reach different informants and might have influenced those who agreed to talk to me. My status as a Congolese man made me appear as an "insider" vis-à-vis the artisanal miners (adults and children) and mine traders, and facilitated the conversation with those who were willing to share their experiences with me. Having previously worked for The Carter Center on a project on child labor trafficking in artisanal mines, I had become acquainted with local NGO workers and human rights activists who shared with me some of their data. Likewise, I had established connections with the law enforcement officers who attended the workshops that I delivered. But, my limited fluency in Swahili disadvantaged me a bit, as some artisanal miners when they heard me speak in French (the DRC's official language) wrongly perceived me as a journalist and refused to be interviewed fearing potential reprisals if their comments or opinions were published in the local media. An NGO worker told me, for instance, that the mining site of Dilala in Kolwezi was closed in mid-2013 by local authorities due in part to the regular publications of journalists and human rights activists denouncing the occurrence of child labor at that site. Furthermore, owing to the situation of insecurity, all the mining sites I visited and the interviews that I conducted were held in areas under the control of the DRC government rather than mining zones controlled by militias and other rebel groups.

Nevertheless, almost none of the child miners whom I interviewed saw themselves as victims of labor exploitation. It was the same for those who employed or sourced from these children; rather than exploitation, they consider themselves as helping the children to earn some money. In the context of generalized poverty, poor families living in the mining regions are forced to work with their children in artisanal and small-scale mines as a principal source of revenue.[8] Community norms influence children to work to contribute to the household's income rather than attend school.[9] The lack of free education also leads children to work in the mines. Despite these socioeconomic factors driving children into mines, it is obvious that child mining labor is one of the worst forms of child labor and a heinous violation of children's rights. It generates profit through depriving children of their childhood, their potential and their dignity, and by harming their physical and mental development.[10]

In this book, I endeavor to portray the extent of child labor in the mining sector in the DRC. I equally attempt to highlight the financial side of child mining labor by tracing the supply chains and describing how child mining labor in the DRC is a problem of globalization, especially in this era of high technology. You may wonder why this book only focuses on child mining labor in the DRC rather than extending the geographical scope to all of sub-Saharan Africa or the African Great Lakes region. DRC is the size of a small continent. It is the second largest country in Africa and is as large as all the western European countries combined. More important, the country possesses some of the world's largest deposits of raw ores such as cobalt, coltan, copper, and tin, which are fundamental elements used in the fabrication of the modern electronics we utilize in our daily lives: cell phones, televisions, computers, cars, airplanes, and vacuums, among others. Unfortunately, a significant portion of these raw materials are produced by children subjected to labor exploitation. These children deserve our attention and thoughts, especially when we use our electronic devices. I hope that this book will prompt greater efforts to prevent child labor in the DRC's mines, to protect vulnerable child victims, and to prosecute those benefiting from child labor exploitation.

ACKNOWLEDGEMENTS

This book project could not have materialized without the contributions of the children, men and women who shared their stories with me. I am deeply thankful to each of them.

There are a few individuals to whom I would particularly like to express my gratitude for their support and assistance in preparing this manuscript. I am especially appreciative of my dear friend and wife Casondra for her encouragement and invaluable insights, which enriched this book. I am also grateful to the local data collectors, guides, and Swahili-French translators who helped me across the DRC's province of Katanga throughout my research, and other people who provided priceless insights to me in Congo. I would like to thank each of them: Auguste Mutombo, Elie Danga, Fridolin Kimonge, Celestin Kandondo, Phillipe Mukim, Fred Malemba, Useni Kanondo, Oscar Banzamwilu, Emmanuel Umpula and Alphonse Banza Kifinda.

My appreciations also go to Julia Mongo, Kelly Cooper, and Casondra Turner-Liwanga for their editing skills. I am particularly thankful to Julie Dahlstrom for taking her time to read and comment on the manuscript's drafts; and to Jean-Pierre Mulumba for his comments on the chapter dealing with the financial aspects of child mining. My thanks also go to friends and colleagues from Harvard University, especially Arlan Fuller, Anne Stetson, Charlie Clements, Jacqueline Bhabha, Jennifer Leaning, and Siddharth Kara; and from Boston University's African Studies Center, namely Jennifer Yanco, Linda Heywood, Tim Longman, Fallou Ngom, and Peter Quella for their incommensurable encouragement and support. Finally, I am thankful to Alpha Academic Press for agreeing to publish this book. Thank you all.

CHAPTER ONE

Child Mining Labor - An Overview

A Seven-year-old Child Miner Named Mutunda in Dilala

Dilala is a mining site in Katanga province where artisanal miners take their raw ores to be sorted and washed. It is named after the nearby Dilala River that crosses the site, and is surrounded by numerous mine trading houses (*comptoirs d'achat*) where artisanal miners sell their minerals. When I arrived, I was told about the presence of children in Dilala, but I did not imagine that there would be many children there because it was daytime and children were supposed to be in school. When I reached the mine, I saw over one hundred children working in the midst of adults. Among those child miners, there was a seven-year-old named Mutunda who was at most four and a half feet tall and weighed about fifty-five pounds. He attracted my attention because he was working in the center of the site, and I saw him as I was walking down to the site from a small hill above. When I approached him, I asked him what he was doing. He unenthusiastically told me that he was washing and sifting heterogenite, which is an ore rich in cobalt and copper minerals. He also said that he had begun working in the mines when he was five. He told me that the two young boys working alongside with him, who were about twelve and thirteen years old, were his brothers. It took me about thirty seconds to process what I was hearing from that small boy. But I wanted to hear more from him. I wanted to know where his parents were, why he was not at school that day, and more. Fortunately, Mutunda agreed to share his story with me:

> My father is unemployed, but works as a mine digger (*creuseur*) in an artisanal mine located about ten miles from here. My mother also works in the mine along with my father. And I have nine siblings--five sisters and four brothers.
>
> Since my parents don't earn a lot of money, all my siblings also work in the mines so we can contribute to the household income. They don't go to school anymore because my parents cannot afford to pay school fees for all of us. Until recently, I was the only one in my family who was attending school. I used to go to school in the morning and work in the mine in the afternoon. But two weeks ago, I was expelled from school because my parents did not pay my school fees for the last three months. Now, I work every day from morning to evening, but I usually take a break around noon. Here, my task is to wash and sift ores. Sometimes, I work for the *négociants* (mine traders) who come here to buy minerals from artisanal miners. But most of the time, I work for myself. I sift through the waste of washed minerals looking for remaining mineral that I wash and resell to the traders. I can earn up to $1.75 or $2.00 per day, and I use that money to buy food, clothes and shoes. I don't like working here; I would prefer being at school.

What is Child Labor?

Is Mutunda a victim of child labor? Before answering this question, it is important to understand the concept of childhood.

Who is a Child? Do Child Miners in the DRC Perceive Themselves as Children?

The concept of childhood is legally and socio-culturally constructed. From a legal viewpoint, the United Nations Convention on the Rights of the Child and the African Charter on the Rights and Welfare of the Child define as a human being below the age of eighteen years unless under the law applicable, majority is attained earlier.[11] In the DRC, the definition of a child has evolved over the past decades. The 1950 Juvenile Delinquency Law defined a child as a person under the age of sixteen.[12] This implies that child offenders between sixteen and eighteen years of age were considered as legal adults and subjected to criminal laws applicable to adult offenders. The 1967 Labor Code implicitly perceived children of sixteen and seventeen years old as adults to the extent that they could perform the same nature of work as adult workers, including dangerous and unhealthy work.[13] While defining a child as a person under eighteen years old,[14] the 1987 Family Code established the minimum age for marriage as fifteen years for women and eighteen years for men.[15] A fifteen-year-old girl who got married was legally considered "an emancipated minor,"[16] which granted her the similar rights and obligations as for adults.[17] Today, the Child Protection Law of 2009 (Law 09/001) not only replicated the description of a child as a person under the age of eighteen,[18] but it also prohibited the precocious marriage of all children (girls and boys).[19] The Law 09/001 equally proscribed the application of adult criminal laws to all child offenders by creating juvenile courts for delinquents younger than eighteen years of age.[20] Furthermore, it forbid the employment of all children (including those between sixteen and eighteen years of age) to conduct dangerous work such as mining labor.[21] In short, the Law 09/001 clarified all ambiguities regarding the definition of a child.

Unlike the legal construction whereby an individual's age is a key criteria, the social conception of childhood in the DRC is based on an individual child's capacity or incapacity to engage in certain social roles. Being a child is not necessarily being under age. A child is defined by contradistinction to an adult;[22] meaning that a child is a person who cannot perform adult roles. Engaging in adult roles can consist, for example, of getting married, procreating children, learning essential life skills (e.g., farming or masonry), or taking up employment to support one's family.[23]

Despite its illegality, precocious marriages are recurrent under the customary rules in the DRC. A fourteen-year-old girl who is married under traditional law or is a child-bearer would be perceived as an adult by her family and society; she would be expected to take care of her children and household as adult people do.[24] Likewise, a physically capable young boy who works in the mines to get food money for his siblings would be considered as an adult by his community. Indeed in some mining areas that I visited, the local society approves children's involvement in mining activities. And the non-worker children are sometimes subjected to derogative epithets. NGO workers that I interviewed in Katanga informed me that non-worker children are called *wabulé* (meaning "a weak or useless person" in the Swahili language), in contrast to *mwana-umé* (meaning a "brave child"). The latter term is used to describe children who work in the mines and contribute to the family's household income.[25] Some child miners that I spoke with, particularly those aged between fifteen and eighteen, told me that they see themselves as adults rather than children at the legal sense; and therefore, they do not consider themselves as being exploited. They also conveyed to me that they feel respected and appreciated when they bring or send money to their families.

At the other hand, in such a society where adulthood is defined based on working capacity or marital status, it is unsurprising to encounter a situation where a "socially- noncompliant" adult was treated as a child. This may be the case of a 40-year-old man who is physically capable, but who willingly refuses to work in mines and prefers relying on relatives for his living. Such a man is, although legally an adult person, socially a child person.

Therefore, even if the legal construction of childhood in the DRC has evolved, the social structure of childhood has remained [26]static in some remote areas, as children reach their social adulthood prematurely. This conflictual reality may render the protection of children more complicated to the extent that the local communities who are supposed to implement child protection laws may simply ignore these laws because the child miners are, in fact, adults in their eyes.

Defining Child Labor

Mutunda is a victim of child labor. But not all forms of work executed by children constitute child labor. Child employment, which includes activities such as assisting in a family business or earning pocket money outside of school hours and during school holidays, is considered positive for children.[27] This is because it prepares children to be productive members of society in the future.[28] According to the International Labor Organization (ILO), the term "child labor" refers to work that deprives children of their childhood, their potential, and their dignity, and that harms their physical and mental development.[29] From this definition, child labor involves at least one of the following elements:

- That children combine school attendance with excessively long and heavy work or the work prevents them from attending school;
- That work threatens children's physical, mental, social or emotional well-being; and
- That work violates a nation's legal minimum age for admission to work.[30]

To assess whether or not a particular kind of "work" constitutes "child labor," it is necessary to evaluate the child's age, the duration and severity of work performed, the conditions under which the labor is executed, and the national labor law of the country where the child works.

Numerous countries have adopted laws regulating the age of admission to employment and the working conditions of children. For example, in the United States, children of fourteen and fifteen years of age may be employed outside of school hours in a variety of nonmanufacturing and nonhazardous work under specified conditions.[31] In France,[32] the legal age for employment is set at sixteen years.[33] In Senegal,[34] the minimum age is fixed at fifteen years, but that age can be reduced to twelve years for light work performed with the child's family.[35]

In the context of the DRC, the country's labor laws regulating child employment have progressed throughout the decades. Before the adoption of the

Labor Code of 1967, children younger than fourteen years old could be employed in any job;[36] but the promulgation of the 1967 Labor Code set the minimum age for employment at fourteen years.[37] Inspired by the ILO Convention on the Minimum Age for Admission to Employment of 1973, the DRC's Labor Code of 2002[38] and Law on the Protection of the Child of 2009[39] have subsequently increased the minimum age for employment to sixteen years of age, and also restricted the nature of work to be performed by children.[40] Children who are between sixteen and eighteen years old are prohibited from engaging in dangerous or unhealthy work.[41] The Department of Labor in the DRC has also issued a Ministerial Order regulating the Working Conditions of Children,[42] which describes the types of hazardous activities prohibited for children, which include mining work among others.[43] The rationale of establishing a legal minimum age for employment is that children are more vulnerable because of their young age, their inexperience in the workplace, and their physical and psychological immaturity.[44] It is therefore necessary to protect them against types of works that are harmful to their health and safety.[45]

A more difficult question is whether child labor exists, for example, in the case of a seventeen-year-old child who consents freely to perform mining activities. It should be noted that the existence of a child miner's consent to work in the mines is not a defense for a child employer or those sourcing directly from him. In other words, a child miner's employer would be criminally responsible for a child-labor offense even if the child miner agrees to work in the mines without constraint. The same offense applies even if the child's parents have authorized their child to perform this hazardous labor.

There is no exhaustive list of hazardous works, which are also known as "worst forms of child labor." Article 3 of the ILO Convention against the Worst Forms of Child Labor (No 182) states that:

The term the worst forms of child labor comprises:
  a) All forms of slavery or practices similar to slavery, such as the sale and trafficking of children, debt bondage and serfdom and forced or compulsory labor, including forced or compulsory recruitment of children for use in armed conflict;
  b) The use, procuring or offering of a child for prostitution, for the production of pornography or for pornographic performances;
  c) The use, procuring or offering of a child for illicit activities, in particular for the production and trafficking of drugs as defined in the relevant international treaties;
  d) Work which, by its nature or the circumstances in which it is carried out, is likely to harm the health, safety or morals of children.

From this description of the worst forms of child labor, the ILO Convention No. 182 considers that acts of the worst forms of child labor also encompass other acts of child economic exploitation, such as the sale and trafficking of children, debt bondage, and forced labor. This raises the question as to the parallelism between child labor and forced and bonded labor and child trafficking. It is important to establish the similarity between these different types of child abuses because not only is it appropriate to place the right label on the corresponding abuse, but also some forms of child exploitation are more severely punished than others, particularly in the DRC.

What Is the Parallelism Between Labor Trafficking and Child Labor?

There is no a unique definition of human trafficking or labor trafficking. The commonly accepted definition of trafficking in persons is stated in the 2000 United Nations Protocol to Prevent, Suppress and Punish Trafficking in Persons, Especially Women and Children (also known as the Palermo Protocol).[46] According to Article 3 of the Protocol, trafficking in persons can be understood as:

a) The recruitment, transportation, transfer, harboring or receipt of persons, by means of the threat or use of force or other forms of coercion, of abduction, of fraud, of deception, of the abuse of power or of a position of vulnerability or of the giving or receiving of payments or benefits to achieve the consent of a person having control over another person, for the purpose of exploitation. Exploitation shall include, at a minimum, the exploitation of the prostitution of others or other forms of sexual exploitation, forced labor or services, slavery or practices similar to slavery, servitude or the removal of organs;

b) The consent of a victim of trafficking in persons to the intended exploitation set forth in subparagraph (a) of this article shall be irrelevant where any of the means set forth in subparagraph (a) have been used;

c) The recruitment, transportation, transfer, harboring or receipt of a child for the purpose of exploitation shall be considered "trafficking in persons" even if this does not involve any of the means set forth in subparagraph (a) of this article.

In light of this broad definition of trafficking, labor trafficking can be understood as the recruitment, transportation, transfer, harboring or receipt of persons by means of the threat or other forms of coercion for the purpose of labor exploitation.

The characteristics of labor trafficking include: (1) acquisition, (2) movement, (3) means of coercion; and (4) labor exploitation.

Acquisition

The acquisition of trafficking victims is generally accomplished through one of the following methods: recruitment by former trafficking victims; abdication; sale by family; seduction; or deceit.[47] Concerning labor trafficking in the DRC's mines, the acquisition of child victims is frequently conducted through the means of recruitment by peers and mine traders.

Movement

The movement of trafficked people does not only consist of moving the victim from his country of origin to a destination country while passing through a transit country.[48] Movement can also be internal, occurring within the national borders of the same country from one province/village to another. In this context, the same country can be considered simultaneously as the country of origin, transit, and destination.[49] During my field research in January 2013, I interviewed a group of four child miners at the mine washing site of Dilala. Nine months later, while I was visiting the mine trading houses in Musompo, I recognized this same group of child miners. They told me that they had been brought to Musompo (situated about fifteen miles away from Dilala) by a mine trader. Artisanal miners in the DRC are often transient, moving from one mine to another in search of sites with high-grade ores. Some *creuseurs* (mine diggers) relocate to different mining locations and bring their child miners with them. Because most mines are located in villages that are five to ten miles apart, child miners are required to leave their villages to follow the creuseurs. This situation qualifies as a labor trafficking case because the child miners were moved from their village of origin to a neighboring village for the specific purpose of working in the artisanal mines. The nuance between child labor and child labor trafficking in the context of DRC artisanal mining relates to the movement of child miners from mine X to mine Y.

Means of Coercion

Under the Palermo Protocol, an act of trafficking supposes that the trafficker has used at least one means of coercion, such as abduction, fraud, deception, or abuse of power. This is a condition sine qua non if the trafficking victim is an adult person; meaning that there is no trafficking if the adult victim willingly consents to acts of trafficking. But the absence of means of coercion is not an absolute defense for the trafficker.[50] Rather, the actual consent of the trafficking victim can be nullified by any after-the-fact coercion by the trafficker.[51] This would be the case of an adult mine worker who agreed to work in the mines for eight hours, but is held by force and coerced to perform mining activity for long hours and is not paid as promised.[52] In this example, "the use of force and coercion by the trafficker has invalidated the initial consent of the victim to engage" in mining activities; thus, it is considered as labor trafficking.[53]

In the case of children, the Palermo Protocol presumes that there is child labor trafficking even if none of the means of coercion were employed because a child is considered to be incapable of giving consent.[54] Means of coercion are not mandatory components of child trafficking.[55] Additionally, the consent of parental authorities is irrelevant in the defense to a charge of child trafficking.[56] This is important because, in the DRC context, it means that some children working in a mine may be victims of trafficking, regardless of whether force or coercion is present.

Exploitation

Exploitation is a compulsory element of trafficking. The Palermo Protocol only enumerates the different forms of exploitation rather than defining the term "exploitation" itself. In contrast, in the DRC, Article 58 of the Law 09/001 describes economic exploitation as any form of abuse of children for economic purposes.[57] Abuse concerns in particular the workload compared to the age of child, time and working hours, insufficient or no compensation, obstruction of work in relation to access to education, physical, mental, moral, spiritual and social development of children.[58]

The components of labor or economic exploitation consist of excessive working hours, lack of holidays or breaks, dangerous working conditions, no salary or meager wages, poor accommodations, intimidation, and isolation.[59] This list of components of labor exploitation is not exhaustive and may include many more unlisted elements.

What is Bonded and Forced Labor?

Forced or compulsory labor can be understood as any work that is extorted from a person under the menace of sanction(s) and for which the said person has not offered himself or herself willingly.[60] Forced-labor victims believe that an attempted escape from their situations would result in serious physical harm or the use of legal coercion, such as the threat of deportation if the victim is an illegal immigrant.[61]

Under the UN Supplementary Convention on the Abolition of Slavery, bonded labor or debt bondage is described as "the status or condition arising from a pledge by a debtor of his personal services or of those of a person under his control as security for a debt, if the value of those services as reasonably assessed is not applied towards the liquidation of the debt or the length and nature of those services are not respectively limited and defined."[62] Illustratively, debt bondage is, for example, the condition of a mine worker who receives cash advances from a mine trader to whom he must sell the mined minerals at prices below market value.[63] That miner may also be forced to continue working to repay constantly accumulating debts that are virtually impossible to pay off. [64]

The nuance between the two terms is that forced labor is characterized by compulsion, whether customary or otherwise, [65] while bonded labor is a specific form of forced labor in which the element of compulsion is derived from debt.[66] Nevertheless, the common denominator between child labor, labor trafficking, forced labor, and bonded labor is that they all constitute an "economic slavery" in which the exploiters profit economically from their victims by taking advantage of the position of vulnerability of the victims due to their young age, financial insecurity, or absence of reasonable alternative.

It is vital to distinguish among these different acts, particularly in the situation of the DRC. As I elaborate further in an upcoming section dealing with the state of legislation on child trafficking and child labor in the DRC, Congolese lawmakers have not only criminalized these acts, but have also set different criminal penalties from one act to another. For example, the crime of child (labor) trafficking is punished by up to twenty years of imprisonment;[67] while the crimes of worst forms of child labor, child bonded labor, and child forced labor are identically punished by up to three years of imprisonment.[68]

What about Mining Labor and Child Sexual Abuse?

Labor exploitation often goes hand in hand with sexual abuse. In the DRC, child sexual abuse in artisanal mines is recurrent. Most of the mining camps I visited were surrounded by bars and restaurants, with small brothels in the back. I was told by NGO workers that many young girls work as miners during the day and provide sexual services at night. Their clients are mostly male artisanal miners or mine traders. I wanted to talk with some of those girls by nightly visiting some of the brothels, which are make-shift structures covered with tarp that are scattered around the mining camps. But I could not find anyone who was willing to speak about this prostitution. In the DRC, as in most societies, child sexual abuse is a taboo subject.[69] Local NGO workers that I also interviewed confirmed to me that people are extremely reluctant to discuss topics related to child sex transactions in the DRC's artisanal mines. Nevertheless, I was determined to get a testimony from a female child victim. One morning in early February 2013, a young woman agreed to talk to me. This occurred the day after I had interviewed Mutunda, the seven-year-old-boy in Dilala.

Let me go back a little bit to my meeting with Mutunda. During my interview with Mutunda, I had asked him if I could also speak with his parents because I wanted to get their viewpoints on allowing their young kids to work in the mines. Mutunda agreed and explained to me where his parents' house was located. The following morning, my guide took me to Mutunda's house to interview his parents who are also both artisanal miners. While I was interviewing Mutunda's parents, his twenty-year-old sister, Brigitte, was present in the house. At the end of my conversation with Mutunda's parents, I asked Brigitte if she would like to say anything. Her response was, "Yes, but not here." I thought that perhaps she did not want to speak in front of her parents, and suggested that we could speak somewhere outside of the house. She was very hesitant, but I felt that she had something important or private to tell me. I proposed that she come to my hotel so we could speak privately. My guide explained to her where my hotel was located, and we arranged to meet later the same day after she had finished her shift in the mines. Around 5:00 p.m., Brigitte came and we sat in the hut at my hotel's compound. I ordered a soda for her, and gently asked her what she had wanted to tell me in private. After a long pause, she began to share part of her story:

> Everything started four years ago. I was sixteen years old at that time. The financial situation in my parents' house was going from bad to worse. Often, there was no money to buy food. As "a young woman" I needed body lotion, clothes, and shoes that my parents could not afford to pay for me. Being the oldest child of a family of nine children, I went to work in the mines to make money. Sometimes, I was not making a lot of money with mining. While working there, some men began soliciting sex from me. They were proposing to pay me more than what I was earning from mining activities. Since I needed money, I began to agree to have sex with them. Most of them are artisanal miners and mine traders. I often have sex with them at nighttime when the mine depots are closed and people have left the mines. Sometimes, I sleep with up to five or six men, and I earn up to 20,000 Congolese francs (about eighteen to twenty dollars) per night. My parents were very upset when they found out that I was having sex for money with men in the mines. They scolded me and asked me to stop it. But I did not stop because we are many in the house. And the money that I was earning was also helping all of us. I am now twenty years old, and I would like to stop doing all of that. Having sex with men for money is a risky job because I can get killed at night or get sick. And my family would lose me if that happens to me. I wish I could have a husband who would assist me to financially help my parents and siblings.

The young girls involved in prostitution around artisanal mines do not necessarily work as miners. There are many ordinary girls who work as "prostituted persons" in locations around the mine just to gain money for their families. In some cases, these girls also work as bartenders or waitresses in the bars and restaurants belonging to the mine traders. A Trafficking in Persons report from the US Department of State also revealed cases of child forced prostitution in markets and mining areas in the DRC by organized networks, gangs, and brothel operators.[70]

Masculinity and Role of Girl Children in Artisanal Mines

Artisanal mining in the DRC is dominantly a masculine activity. Women (including those working with or without their spouses or other relatives) represent about twenty percent of the total population of artisanal mining workers in the DRC.[71] In most of the artisanal mines I visited, the number of girl child-miners was relatively the same as of boy child-miners. As discussed in Chapter Three on the working conditions in artisanal mines, children in artisanal mines perform different types of activities: tasks related to mining exploitation (such as extraction, transportation, sifting and cleaning of minerals), and supportive tasks (including selling food, alcohol and cigarettes to artisanal miners). In regard to the mining exploitation's activities, I observed during my visits in the artisanal mines that the duties of female artisanal miners (including girl child-miners) were limited to transporting, sifting, cleaning, or trading minerals.

Photo 1.1 Girl child-miners holding bags containing minerals.

There were literally no female artisanal miners performing as *creuseurs* (mine diggers) in the mine extraction sites. I wondered as to why women were absent as diggers at the mine extracting sites. I thought that it was perhaps due to the fact that female artisanal miners were not interested in performing such a physically demanding and dangerous task as digging several feet underground to extract minerals. But when I asked people at the artisanal mines about such an absence of female miners at the mine extraction sites, I was told that women are in general prohibited by male artisanal miners from approaching the places where minerals are extracted. This is because there is a superstitious belief among artisanal miners that the presence of women in the extraction sites could cause the disappearance of minerals or the lowering of the ores' grades.[72] Ores such as cobalt are categorized as high-grade or low-grade;[73] high-grade minerals are more expensive than the low-grade ones.[74] As earlier mentioned, artisanal miners in Katanga constantly move from one mine to another searching for high-grade ores, which have more value. Of course there is no causality between the difficulty for male artisanal miners of finding high-grade ores and the presence of women at the mine extracting sites. As described in Chapter Three, the challenge for artisanal miners in gaining access to high-grade ores is most likely caused by their lack of geological information on the mining lands and the lack of adequate technology to enable them to assess in advance the quality of ores in the zones where they are plan to dig.[75] Local NGO workers that I spoke to about the issue of the absence of women at the mine extraction sites, told me that such an exclusion of women from places where mines are extracted also reflect the existing culture of gender discrimination in the DRC.[76] Indeed, researchers have concluded that Congolese women face gender inequality in all domains of life, including socioeconomic and political.[77] An illustration of such gender discrimination can also be found within the provisions of the DRC Mining Code[78] that deal with the ineligibility from conducting mining activities. In light of Article 27(b) of the Mining Code, married women are ineligible to have artisanal miners' cards or traders' card to conduct mining activities in the DRC without the authorization of the spouses.[79] In reality, many artisanal miners (female and male) that I met with did not possess artisanal miners' cards.[80]

However in a mining site called PUIT 7 in Kupushi, I found some female artisanal miners digging minerals alongside with male miners. That was a bit surprising for me. But I assumed that the only reason for their presence was because the PUIT 7 mine is actually a zone waste area where artisanal miners come to collect the waste of zinc-copper minerals dumped by Gecamines, a state-owned mining company. Considering the high risk associated with the mining digging task, the *creuseurs* (mine diggers) who work underground earn three times more than their colleagues who work on the surface and execute only tasks of transporting, sifting, and cleaning minerals.[81] Excluding female artisanal miners from performing the digging task, which is highly well-compensated, can therefore reinforce economic discrimination of women based on their gender, as they can only execute low-paid tasks in the artisanal mines.

What of Armed Conflicts and Mining Activities?

The DRC experienced a nearly decade-long armed conflict from the late 1990s to the early 2000s during which over four to five million people died as a result of conflict, three million people were displaced within the DRC, two million fled the country to seek asylum in the neighboring States, and several hundred thousand were subjected to inhuman treatments and destruction of property.[82] About eight foreign national armies and dozens of local and foreign armed groups were involved in what is also known as the Great African War or African World War.[83] According to the UN Panel of Experts, foreign national armies and different armed groups participating in the DRC's conflict frequently sought to control mining lands to illegally exploit minerals (such as tantalum, tin, tungsten and gold) to finance their military activities.[84] Additionally, a report from the US's Department of State also disclosed that these armed groups forcibly recruited children not only to serve as soldiers in battle, but also to work in the artisanal mines as conscript laborers.[85] During my field research, I only visited mining zones under the control of the DRC government and where armed groups were not operational. Despite only visiting artisanal mines located in the no-war areas, I observed children working in some mining lands that were protected by regular soldiers and police officers.

Who Employs Children?

An overwhelming majority of child miners in the DRC work for their parents or themselves rather than working for mining companies or engaging in other forms of wage employment in the mining industry.

Employers	Number of children by percent
Family (including parents, uncles/aunts and brothers/sisters)	53%
Self-employment	18.5%
Friends	18.5%
Others (including mine traders and adult artisanal miners)	5%

Table 1.1: Employers of Child Miners in Katanga

Source: Author's Estimates.

Table 1.1. represents the results of a survey that I conducted of sixty-three child workers in artisanal mining sites in the DRC's province of Katanga between January and February 2013. It provides some context of who child miners work for in the mines. According to my research, about 53% of the child miners worked for or with their family members, 18.5% worked for themselves, and another 18.5% worked for friends. What is a bit surprising is that only 5% of the child miners worked for mine traders or unrelated adult miners. These statistics should not, however, be perceived as representing the scale of the problem in Katanga or DRC alone. According to a 2001–2002 research project conducted by UNICEF in low-income countries around the world, most working children are employed by their parents instead of by manufacturing establishments.[86]

Child miners, who work with their family members labor as part of the family business, help to increase the family's profits.[87] These children start working in the mines by accompanying their parents or siblings; they quickly learn how to amass small amounts of waste ores around the artisanal mining sites or dig for minerals.[88] Their collected minerals are mixed with those of other family members and the proceeds of those minerals serve as their contribution to the family's household income.[89] Children working for adult artisanal miners who are not part of their family perform tasks assigned to them and get paid either a flat daily per diem or for a fraction of the minerals produced.[90] Those who work for mine traders are usually supplied with tools or advanced cash from the traders to whom they sell their mined minerals.[91] If the children don't harvest minerals equivalent to the amount of advanced cash, the traders require them to continue working to repay the debt.[92] Child miners who work for themselves are generally more independent as they are free to sell their products directly to traders and to get paid based on the quantity (weight) and quality (grade) of minerals sold. There are also cases where traders purchase mined minerals from artisanal miners and pay them with food rather than money. In this case, the traders provide artisanal miners with rice, sugar, oil, flour or other products in exchange for minerals.

It should be noted, however, that even though most child miners in the DRC do not work for mining companies, nearly all of the mined minerals harvested by child miners are purchased by mining companies and smelters either directly or indirectly. I further elaborate on the supply chains of child-mined minerals in Chapter Four.

What Is the State of Legislation on Child Trafficking and Child Labor in the DRC?

The DRC has ratified numerous international instruments against human trafficking and child exploitation, such as the UN Convention against Transnational Organized Crime and its Protocol on the Prevention, Suppression and Punishment of Trafficking in Persons (Palermo Protocol), the UN Convention against the Worst Forms of Child Labor, and the UN Convention on the Minimum Age for Admission to Employment. In ratifying those instruments, specifically the Palermo Protocol, the DRC government has, among other things, committed to adopt comprehensive legislation to combat all forms of human trafficking.[93]

But the DRC has not yet adopted a comprehensive anti-trafficking law at the domestic level.[94] Instead, it has provisions within its laws that condemn certain aspects of trafficking in persons.[95] For instance, the Law 06/018 of July 2006 amending the Penal Code[96] criminalizes pimping,[97] forced prostitution,[98] child prostitution,[99] and sexual slavery.[100] Although that Law does not explicitly mention the word "sex trafficking," its definition of sex slavery is broad enough to contain attributes of trafficking for sexual exploitation.[101] The DRC's Penal Code lacks provisions dealing with trafficking for non-sexual forms of exploitation.[102] However, the country's Labor Code of 2002[103] has provisions proscribing forced or compulsory labor,[104] the worst forms of child labor,[105] and child bonded labor.[106] Yet, the Labor Code is "silent" about bonded labor offenses committed against adult victims.[107] This silence of the Labor Code on adult bonded labor, combined with the disregard of the Penal Code to non-sexual forms of trafficking, creates a kind of "legal insecurity" against adult victims of debt bondage who are unprotected by the law.[108]

In 2009, the DRC passed the Child Protection Law (Law 09/001). This law contains the only explicit definition of human trafficking (whether child or adult) in the country's domestic legal arsenal. The scope of that definition is solely limited to child trafficking to the extent that Article 162(2)(1) of the Law 09/001 stipulates that "child trafficking is the recruitment, transportation, transfer, harboring or receipt of children, by means of the threat or use of force or other forms of coercion, of abduction, of fraud, of deception, of the abuse of power or of a position of vulnerability or of the giving or receiving of payments or benefits to achieve the consent of a person having control over children for the purpose of exploitation."

Law 09/001 also proscribes the sale and trafficking of children,[109] as well as the worst forms of child labor,[110] debt bondage,[111] compulsory labor,[112] and forced military recruitment of children.[113]

Recognizing the prevalence of child labor in the mining sector, the DRC enacted the 2002 Mining Code regulating mining exploitation in the country. The DRC Mining Code contains some provisions that tacitly deal with child labor by listing children in the catalogue of persons ineligible for conducting mining activities,[114] including extracting, washing, sifting, transporting, or selling minerals. The Mining Code also sets economic penalties for illegal mining activities[115] and unlawful purchase/sale of minerals,[116] which may be extended to cases of buying child-labor minerals or involving children in mining activities.

In 2013, the DRC government also approved a National Action Plan that aimed to eradicate all the worst forms of child labor by 2020. The National Plan is an essential instrument to the extent that it defines the government's approach and priority actions to fight the scourge of dangerous child labor at all sectors. Unfortunately, the implementation of this National Plan has been very slow since its adoption.

In conclusion, the DRC's anti-human trafficking provisions are fragmented by nature, and some of the practical implications of such legal fragmentation include the difficulty of enforcement owing to the limited operational scope of the laws, and the uneven enforcement of the laws due to the lack of harmony of different provisions.[117] In the context of child labor, the problem hinges more on the implementation of the existing child protection provisions rather than the inherent weakness of the laws themselves.

CHAPTER TWO

Root Causes of Child Labor in the Mines

As in numerous African countries and other parts of the globe, child labor in the DRC is not a contemporary phenomenon. Historically, African children were also involved in the labor force during the pre-colonial and colonial periods, principally in the agricultural and domestic sectors.[118] The child labor that occurred before colonization was predominantly driven by sociocultural reasons;[119] children in rural areas were required to work with their parents to learn essential life skills or to acquaint themselves with various methods of farming in order to become successful adults in the future.[120] Later, with the exposure to monetarization and industrialization, child labor transformed from life skills learning into economic exploitation.[121] This practice of child labor also continued under colonial rule where children in the DRC were, for instance, forcibly employed in rubber farms and physically abused whenever they failed to produce the requested quota of products that were destined for exportation.[122] Even though there are still a significant number of children working in agricultural, domestic and other sectors, the modern-day and prevalent form of child labor in the DRC largely consists of children working in the mining sector.[123] There are several combined factors that contribute to today's child mining labor in the DRC including poverty, adult unemployment, lack of educational opportunities, sociocultural variables, lack of law enforcement, and the globalization with high demand for mined minerals.

Poverty, Unemployment and Credit Constraints

Global studies conducted in most parts of the world, including Europe and the United States, have shown that the poorer a family is, the more likely its children are to work.[124] In analyzing the census data for Philadelphia, economist Claudia Goldin also concluded that, "The higher the father's wage, the lower the probability of the child participating in labor force....The father's unemployment sends both boys and girls into the labor force."[125]

As shown in Table 2.1. on a poverty index the DRC ranks 228 out of 228 on the list of countries by GDP (gross domestic product) per capita. About 71% of its population lives on less than $1.25 per day. The Table also indicates an additional 15.1 % of the DRC's population is vulnerable to multiple deprivations while the intensity of deprivation, which is the average percentage of deprivation experienced by people living in multidimensional poverty,[126] is estimated at 53% of the population.

Country	GDP Rank	Head count (%)	Intensity of deprivation (%)	Population			Education				Un-employ-ment
				Vulnerable to poverty (%)	In severe poverty (%)	Below income poverty line (%)	Pre-primary school participation, Gross enrolment ratio (%)	Primary school participation, Net attendance ratio (%)	Secondary school participation, Net attendance ratio (%)	Child- out-of- school	
DRC	228	71	53	15.1	45.9	87.7	3.6	74.5	32.5	7.3M	73
Nigeria	180	54.1	57.3	17.8	33.9	68	14	70	54	-	37.7
Ethiopia	211	87.3	64.6	6.8	71.1	39	5.3	87	15.5	-	18

Table 2.1: Countries Poverty Index

Source for unemployment data: African Economy Outlook.
Source for education data: UNICEF.
Source for GDP data: US Central Intelligence Agency (CIA).
Source for all other data: World Bank.

Additionally, more than 73% of the DRC's active population is unemployed, which may contribute for the country's inclusion in the list of nations with the largest share of the global extreme poor. Figure 2.1. indicates that as of 2010, about 5% of the world's 1.2 billion extreme poor lived in the DRC. Other countries home to the global extreme poor include India (33%), China (13%), Nigeria (9 %), and Bangladesh (5%).

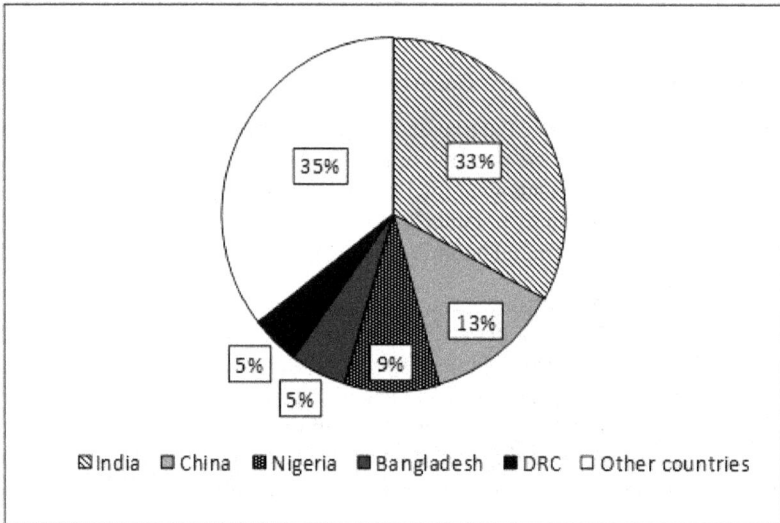

Figure 2.1: List of Countries Sharing Global Extreme Poverty, 2010 (Percent)
Source: United Nations-The Millennium Development Goals Report.

In this context of extreme poverty in the DRC, poor families living in the mining regions often encourage their children to work in the mines to help contribute to the household's income. Children are led to believe that they must work in solidarity with their family members to compensate as much as possible for the family's economic burden.[127] Even the meager monetary contributions of children are treasured in the poverty-stricken households in which they abide.[128]

Some authors argue that credit constraints can lead to an increase in child labor: Because the poorest households are unable to access the well-functioning credit and insurance markets, they are forced to send their children to work.[129] Researchers have noted that 71% of households in the DRC, particularly farm households, endure credit constraints.[130]

Lack of Educational Structure

Based on my interviews with child miners and other informants in the DRC mines, the lack of educational structure is another reason why many children work in the DRC's mines. The DRC constitution guarantees free and compulsory primary education for every child[131] and the government has set a goal of achieving education for all children by 2015. Unfortunately, these constitutional provisions are not fully enforced. There are no schools in most remote mining areas and, where schools exist, primary education is often not free. In fact, some school authorities whom I spoke with told me that although the government was supposed to pay school teachers' salaries, it often fails to do so. Therefore, primary school-aged children, or their parents, are required to pay teachers' salaries and school operating costs in both private and public schools. If they cannot pay, they are forced out of the school.

As Table 2.1. indicates, in 2008–2011 about 74% of children were attending primary school in the DRC, and 35.5% were enrolled in secondary school. These numbers demonstrate that there has been significant progress in the DRC in terms of the rate of child school attendance; from 1996–2002 only 64% and 21% of children were respectively attending primary and secondary schools.[132] Despite that progress, there are still about 7.3 million Congolese school-age children (representing about 14% of the entire country's population) who do not attend school.

Figure 2.2. represents the school expenditures in the DRC, which are the total public expenditure per student in primary and secondary education as a percentage of GDP per capita.[133] The public expenditure includes government spending on educational institutions (both public and private), education administration, and subsidies for private entities.[134]

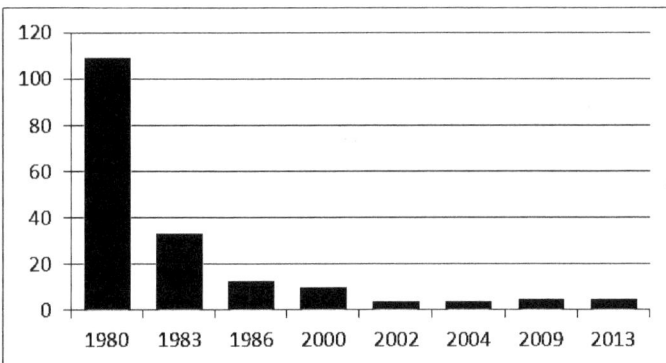

Figure 2.2: School Expenditures in the DRC in USD
Source: Author's estimates based on World Bank data.

The graph shows that school expenditures in the DRC decreased from $109 per student per year in 1980 to $4.90 per student per year in 2013. This implies that there was an average decrease of $38 of school expenditures every ten years. In other words, total school expenditures in the DRC decreased 34.5% per decade during this thirty-year period. If this trend continues, school expenditures in the DRC may be barely existent by 2025.

Table 2.2. shows yearly education fees for each primary school student in the DRC's public schools as of 2003. The Table indicates that each primary school student was required to pay school fees averaging between $23 and $145 per year; meaning that the average education fees in public schools were about $85 per student per year in 2003. This amount may surely double by the time you read this book owing to the inflationary cost of living in the DRC. Nevertheless, even $85 per primary school student appears a bit excessive in the DRC where 71% of the population lives on less than $1.25 per day. This situation is even direr for families who have more than one school-aged child. Most families in the DRC have an average of 4.8 children.[135]

Provinces	School Fees				Total in $
	Tuitions in $	Teacher Wages in $	Functioning Fees in $	Ad-hoc Intervention Fees in $	
Bas Congo	1.20	34.60	24.30	7.56	67.66
Bandundu	1.20	30.80	11.40	5.20	48.60
Equateur	1.20	13.30	12.60	5.60	32.70
Kasai Occidental	1.20	12.40	9.60	---	23.20
Kasai Oriental	1.20	15.70	12.60	---	29.50
Katanga	1.20	30.20	13.20	17.40	62
Kinshasa (The Capital city)	1.20	93	24	26.60	144.80

Table 2.2: Education Fees per Primary School Student per Year in Public Schools in the DRC: 2003
Source: Author's calculations based on World Bank data.

Furthermore, more than 50% of students' school fees are used to cover teacher wages. The tuition itself represents approximately less than 5% of the total fees that students are required to pay. As noted above, the students, or their parents, are required to pay teacher salaries in public schools because the DRC's government often fails to do so. A report from PACT, a developmental NGO, revealed that even when the government was paying teachers' salaries, the wage was too low to provide a decent living.[136] Some schools were forced to collect additional fees from parents, and some teachers in the mining provinces, such as Katanga, went to work in artisanal mines to supplement their incomes.[137] Moreover, school fees are not uniform in all public schools across the DRC. According to Table 2.2. school fees are higher in the major urban cities (such as Kinshasa) than in other provinces or rural areas. Many child miners that I interviewed in the rural mining areas told me that they combine working in the mines and attending school, by using some of the money they earn towards paying their education fees, which are expensive for them. Other child miners have simply dropped out of school because, with the extreme poverty in which they are living, payment of education fees is not a priority for their families.[138]

Sociocultural Factors

Child labor not only reflects on economic situations but also depends on the normative attitudes of the community towards children.[139] As earlier discussed, the participation of children in mining activities is tolerated by some communities in the mining regions to the extent that child mining has almost become a social norm. In Chapter One, I elaborated that some local communities in Katanga use the derogative epithet of *wabulé* (meaning "useless person" in the Swahili language) to describe the non-child miners. Thus, to avoid the denigratory label of *wabulé* and gain the complimentary sobriquet of *mwana-umé* (a term meaning "brave child" and used to describe working children),[140] some children get involved in mining labor so that they can prove their bravery.

Child-witchcraft Accusations

Child-witchcraft accusation is a phenomenon that tends to increase the number of children in the mines in different ways. Many children are rejected or abandoned by their families because their parents, traditional healers, or church leaders believe that these children are possessed by *kindoki,* a black magic power.[141] These children are thought to be possessed by witchcraft because they are believed to be the cause of, for instance, a family member's unemployment, inability to get married, contamination with sickness, or involvement in a tragic accident or death. Sometimes, people don't understand that their illnesses are caused by pathogens; instead, they try to find a scapegoat for their misfortunes.[142] The accusation of witchcraft often falls on children, particularly those who show signs of malnutrition, pale appearance, protruding belly, or disobedience to parents, among other things.[143] Good-looking children from rich families are rarely accused of kindoki.

Lack of Legal Enforcement

The impunity of child-labor offenders permits the persistence of child labor in the DRC's mines. Despite the fact that provisions of the Law on Child Protection respectively punish cases of child trafficking with imprisonment up to twenty years,[144] and cases of the worst forms of child labor with imprisonment up to three years,[145] no single prosecution has ever been initiated against child-labor offenders.[146] There are three reasons that may explain the impunity of perpetrators of child mining labor offences, namely:

1) Lack of sufficient training and the means to investigate and prosecute child labor offenders. Many law enforcement officers, principally child labor investigators or inspectors, often lack means of transportation or resources to carry out their work in remote mining areas.[147]

2) Lack of judicial independence and corruption within the justice system. Many child-mining labor offenders are not prosecuted because they bribe the judicial officers assigned to conduct investigation of the cases. Other offenders are the *protégés* of influential political leaders or high-ranked prosecutors and judges who in turn put pressure on the low-ranked law enforcement officers investigating the case.

During my research, I video-interviewed one of the prosecutors at the *Parquet de Grande Instance* (Office of the Public Prosecutor) in Lubumbashi who told me that while he was aware of cases of child labor in the mines, he did not investigate because he never received any formal complaints or denunciations from the victims. I was shocked and disappointed to hear from a prosecutor such a justification of lack of law enforcement based on an argument that is not absolutely true from a legal point of view. In fact, the provisions of the DRC Code of Judicial Organization and Competence allow prosecutors to initiate investigations either by receiving complaints/denunciations or by their own initiative for any infringements that they have knowledge of.[148] The prosecutor is not supposed to wait for formal complaints before investigating child mining labor cases as long as he has knowledge that offenses are being committed. However, I abruptly comprehended that this prosecutor was reluctant to reveal during the recorded interview his real reason for not prosecuting child labor offenders. As soon as I turned the camera off, he literally told me: "Here, one does not prosecute for the sake of prosecuting; one should first know who is behind that…" In other words, the prosecutor wanted to say that before investigating or prosecuting child labor offenders, it is important to find out whether or not those offenders are benefiting from the protection of government officials or highly-ranked prosecutors and judges. This is because if one "mistakenly" prosecutes an "untouchable offender" with strong political connections, then one would probably face reprisals.

3) Conflict between the need to survive vs. the application of the rule of law: A Head Judge from a *Tribunal de Paix* (Tribunal of Peace) whom I interviewed informed me that some law enforcement officers weigh the child's best interests in opting not to prosecute parents who exploit the labor of their own children. The fact is that convicting child miners' parents might render children as "quasi-orphans" in a country where the government lacks programs to provide shelters or other basic assistance to needy children. Also, if a prosecution is initiated, there might not be alternative viable means for the child or family to support themselves.

Globalization and High Demand for Mined Minerals

The high demand for mined minerals is another factor that contributes to child labor in the DRC's mining sectors. During the last decade, there has been a growing demand for raw ores; particularly those that are fundamental elements for the electronic, automobile, aeronautic, and chemical industries. These raw materials are very often transferred from developing countries, including the DRC, to developed nations and regions such as the United States, European Union, Canada, Japan, and others. Figure 2.3. represents the worldwide production of cobalt from 2008 to 2012. The graph shows that cobalt production increased from 72,000 tons in 2008 to 110,000 tons in 2012. This means that there was an average increase of 7,600 tons of cobalt production each year, meaning that total cobalt production increased 7% per annum during this five-year period. If this trend continues, cobalt production may well reach 145,000 tons per year by 2017.

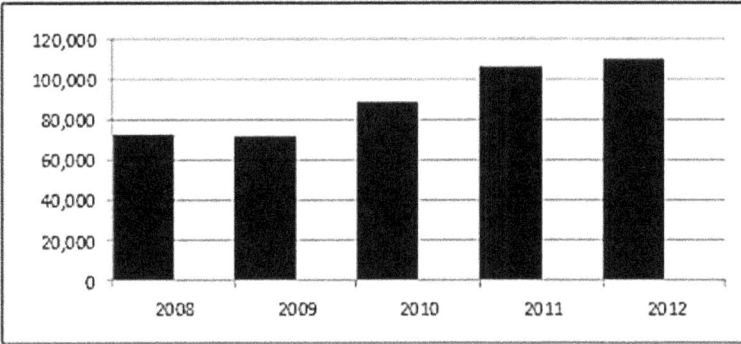

Figure 2.3: Worldwide Cobalt Mine Production from 2008 to 2012 (Tons metric)
Source: US Geological Survey-Mineral Resources Program.

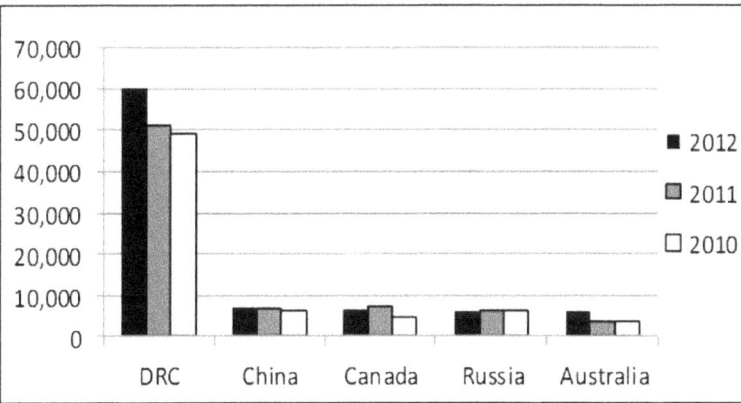

Figure 2.4: Cobalt Mine Production per Country from 2010 to 2012 (Tons metric)
Source: US Geological Survey-Mineral Resources Program.

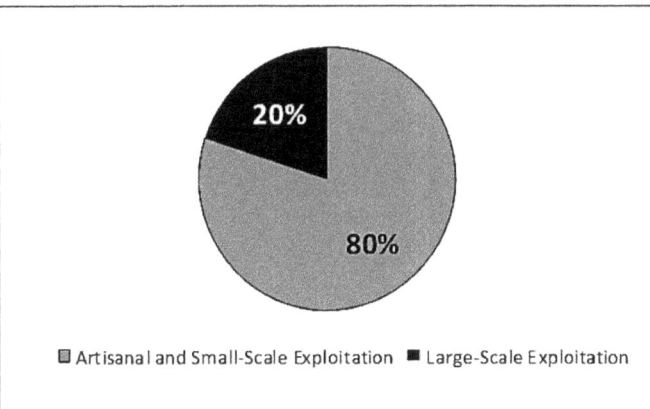

Figure 2.5: DRC Cobalt Mine Exploitation by Operational Scale
Source: Author's Estimates from World Bank data.

As background information, the mining sector in the DRC currently accounts for about 12% of the country's GDP.[149] Before the liberalization of the mining sector through the adoption of the 2002 Mining Code, state-owned mining companies in the DRC had a monopoly of mining exploitation in the country.[150] With the adoption of the new Mining Code, the monopoly of state-owned companies was suppressed, private mining companies were authorized to operate, and artisanal mining exploitation was legally recognized.[151] Technically, mining exploitation in the DRC is now divided into two large sectors.[152] On the one hand, there is large-scale or industrial exploitation, which is dominated by state-owned and private companies that use industrial and modern mining methods.[153] On the other hand, there is artisanal and small-scale exploitation that uses rudimentary methods to extract and process mined minerals; this sector is principally dominated by artisanal miners.[154] Despite the use of traditional means of exploitation, artisanal mining is "the largest segment of the DRC mining sector and the one that has the highest impact in terms of production as well as persons involved."[155] With the exception of copper and cobalt, which are exploited through both industrial and artisanal mining, most mined minerals in the DRC are produced by artisanal and small-scale mining.[156] According to World Bank estimates, 90% of all mineral production in the DRC comes from artisanal miners.[157] There is a lack of official statistics on the number of people involved in artisanal mining in the DRC. One of the reasons explaining the difficulty of identifying all artisanal miners is that most of them do not possess artisanal miner cards as required by law. Articles 111 and 112 of the Mining Code oblige artisanal miners to obtain valid cards from local mining authorities prior to conducting mining activities; but very few of them hold those cards. Nevertheless, the World Bank estimates that the number of all active artisanal miners (both adults and children) in the DRC is somewhere between 500,000 to 2,000,000 persons, and the number of people whose livelihood depends on artisanal mining activity could be as high as eight to ten million,[158] representing 14% to 16% of the total population of the DRC.[159] In relation to cobalt production in the DRC, it is estimated that there are about 100,000 to 150,000 people working in the cobalt artisanal mines in the DRC,[160] of which 40,000 to 50,000 are children.[161]

With the global economy characterized by growing demand for mined minerals and cheap labor, there is today a high prevalence of child labor in the DRC's mines as compared to two decades ago when the presence of children in the mines was very low.[162] Siddharth Kara, a colleague of mine and a worldwide respected human trafficking expert, has noted: "The most effective way for any business to increase profits is to minimize costs. For most business, the largest operating cost is labor."[163] In the DRC, the monthly salary of an adult miner employed by a state-owned mining company, such as Gécamines, is roughly between $45 and $225 (about $1.50 to $7.50 per day)[164] whereas the average earning of most children working in the cobalt artisanal mines varies from $0.75 to $3.00 per day.[165] Thus, child labor is very profitable for mine traders and corporations.

CHAPTER THREE

Working Conditions and Fate of Child Miners

A Conversation with *Creuseurs* in an Open-Pit Mine in Musonoi

Photo 3.1: Open-pit mine of Musonoi.

In that warm morning of 2013, I climbed an estimated terrain of 1,459 meters (about 4,787 feet) above sea level[166] to reach the peak of an open-pit mine in Musonoi. There, I saw many groups of *creuseurs* (mine diggers) who were digging for ores at different places. Each group of miners that I met had at least two members. One of the first *creuseurs* I spoke with on that day was named Marco. When I saw him, Marco was holding an iron shovel of about four feet long next to a hole that was seven or nine feet deep. What was a bit strange was that Marco was working alone; I did not see anyone else around him. I was intrigued and approached him to inquire if I could ask him some questions, to which he gently agreed. Our conversation was held concurrently in both French and Swahili.

"How old are you?" I asked.

"Fifteen years old," he responded.

"What is the tool that you are holding?"

"A shovel."

"What do you use it for?"

"To dig up to extract ores."

"But the hole you are digging is getting quite deep. Aren't you concerned that it can be dangerous for you if you get in and keep digging further?

"Yes, I know that. But, as you can see, I started to prepare and create rooms inside of the hole before carrying on with digging."

"How can you further dig while you are working alone?"

"No, I am not really alone. I work with my uncle. He is over there, the other side of the mine. He will come back to join me."

In speaking about the "rooms" inside of the hole, Marco was referring to corridors that miners usually create underground when they reach some depth; these corridors may be connected with other holes underground. But I do not understand any correlation between the digging of these underground corridors and the prevention and protection of miners against soil collapse.

About two hundred feet from Marco's mining hole, there was another group of three *creuseurs* who had just started to dig another hole. They were digging in a rocky spot and their hole was about five feet deep and six feet in diameter. They told me that they had only been digging for a couple of hours; but they seemed to me very tired as if they had already worked for the entire day. I jokingly asked one of those miners, the one who was on the surface, if I could help them to dig. He looked at me, smiled, and said "yes" while nodding. He told his colleague who was working at the bottom of the hole to get out, and to leave the iron pick that he was using inside of the hole. I told them that I was only joking, but they insisted that I should try. And I agreed. I jumped inside of that rocky hole with the pair of jeans and climbing shoes that I was wearing on that day. Once inside the hole, I picked up their iron pick and was surprised at how heavy it was. The pick weighed somewhere between twenty-five and thirty-five pounds. After digging for about only one or two minutes, I felt really exhausted and was sweating from everywhere. I also felt a bit suffocated in that hole where the air circulation was deficient. It was truly painful. When I got out, all the *creuseurs* were smiling. But I did not ask them why. I do not think that their smiles were intended to mock me. Their smiles were meant to convey how difficult mining truly was. It was a way for them to find solidarity in the back-breaking nature of their work.

Later that evening, while I was in my hotel room, I took some pain killers and thought about my mining experience that day. I remember thinking to myself, if an adult person such as I could get quickly exhausted for only mining less than five minutes, then what about the child diggers who work more than ten hours per day?

Working Conditions in the Artisanal Mines

Artisanal mining in the DRC is characterized by poor working conditions. In all of the artisanal mining sites that I visited, I noticed a poor level of mechanization and a lack of minimum standards of health and security. I observed many child miners working with bare hands and feet, and without protective gear.

In artisanal mines, the extraction of mined minerals is done by hand with picks, shovels, and buckets. Artisanal miners are required by law not to dig more than thirty meters (ninety-eight feet) underground to extract ores.[167] But, some artisanal miners excavate up to 140 meters (460 feet) in tunnels that regularly lack any form of structural support.[168]

Photo 3.2: A child miner sitting next to a mining hole

Photo 3.2. shows a child miner sitting next to a mining hole. Generally, most of these deep tunnels experience a problem of insufficient ventilation which may expose diggers to the risk of asphyxia; and in rare cases, artisanal miners use small pumps to allow for ventilation of air.[169] Mine diggers work in groups of at least two people. Usually, there is at least one miner who digs for ores with a shovel or pick at the bottom of the hole while the other miners pull ores to the surface by using a bucket attached to a long string. Some NGO workers that I interviewed told me that children are principally tasked to dig because their small sizes facilitate crawling into those narrow holes.

Artisanal miners often use mercury to isolate ores, particularly in gold mining.[170] In order to purify gold, artisanal miners usually blend ores dug from the ground or from stream beds with mercury to form an amalgam.[171] When the amalgam is burned, the mercury vaporizes into a toxic cloud while the gold remains behind.[172] Furthermore, artisanal miners regularly use heavy metal tools to crush rock or metallic ores, such as coltan and cobalt. In some sites that I visited, such as *Terre Jaune* near Kolwezi, I discovered artisanal miners also using an obsolete crushing machine to crush rocks.

Photo 3.3: A child miner transporting a bag containing mined minerals.

Photo 3.3. displays a child miner transporting a bag containing mined minerals on his shoulder. Commonly, artisanal miners transport their mined minerals on their heads or shoulders from the mines to the washing sites or from the washing sites to the depots, depending on the distance.[173] In some cases, artisanal miners also use bicycles to transport their minerals. Children, whose tasks include carrying ores, are called "saliseurs" or "transporteurs" or "porteurs."[174]Saliseurs can carry loads of minerals weighing up to fifty or sixty kilograms (about one hundred or 120 pounds) for many miles.

Photo 3.4: A group of three child miners washing and sifting mined

Photo 3.4. shows a group of three child miners cleaning the mined minerals. The washing of ores is conducted either in a river nearby the mines or in big tanks filled with water where there is no river or lake in the vicinity of the mines. Children who perform the cleaning of minerals are called "*laveurs*" (washers).[175] They also execute the sifting of ores by using sieves, metallic mesh, or sieves made out of a plastic barrel. It should be noted that artisanal miners also use the same river water for their personal bathing, washing clothes and dishes, and cooking.[176]

Impacts of Mining Activities on Children?

Artisanal mining is characterized by the lack of a minimum standard of health and security, which is particularly harmful to the physical, mental and behavioral development of children.

Physical impacts

The physical effects of mining on children consist of injuries, sicknesses, developmental problems, and fatal accidents which are inherent to the dangerous working conditions.[177] Child miners are exposed to greater risks of having their physiological development hampered than non-working children because of their contact with dangerous substances and exposure to accidents and physical stress.[178]

Mother of a dead child miner in Musonoi mine

Three weeks after the sudden death of Zadio, a thirteen-year-old boy who was engulfed in a mining hole, I met with his thirty-four-year-old mother Hortense. That day, I was routinely conducting interviews and had an appointment with some NGO workers whose office was located not far from the Musonoi mine. Towards the end of my interview with these NGO workers, I asked them about cases of accidents in the artisanal mines. One of them said to me, "Actually, there was a case of child death in the Musonoi mine three weeks ago…I know the family of that deceased child." I asked him if he could facilitate a meeting between me and the child's parents. Hours later, while I was still conducting more interviews with other child miners in the Musonoi mine, the NGO worker called to inform me that he was coming to fetch me from the mine because Hortense, the mother of the deceased child miner, had agreed to speak with me. In that moment, I was quietly thinking how I would begin the conversation with Hortense, a woman grieving over the death of her young son. When the NGO worker came, he took me to Hortense's house, which was located around the corner from the mine. From Hortense's house, I could even see people going to and working in the mine. The mine was a kind of "backyard" of her home.

When I arrived at Hortense's house, she greeted me and my accompaniers and asked us to sit on chairs. But she sat herself on the floor, symbolizing that she was still mourning her son. According to the local tradition, the forty-day mourning period after her son's death had not yet passed. I told Hortense that I was a researcher and would like to talk with her about her son and how he died. With a voice full of sorrow, she said "fine," and started to tell her part of the story:

> The day of his death, Zadio went to work in the Musonoi mine with his two friends as usual. Around 10:00 a.m., one of his friends came to inform us that there was a soil collapse and that Zadio was engulfed underground. Zadio was the one who was digging while his friends were on the surface pulling the bucket containing ores. My heart was broken and I ran to the mine where the situation occurred. When I got there, I found other artisanal miners trying to remove the dirt to get him out. It took them about three hours to take him out. It was very late, and Zadio was already dead. My Zadio was only thirteen years old and had just passed to fifth grade. He died owing to the difficulty of life. I remember two weeks before his death; he was working all the time in the mine because he wanted to get money to buy school uniforms and other items, given that the beginning of the school year was approaching. He even bought himself a school uniform and some notebooks. But now, he died and did not even use everything that he had already bought. It is heartbreaking. Since Zadio's death, I have been preventing his young brother from working in the mines. I don't want to lose another child.

Death in artisanal mines

Numerous artisanal miners are exposed to the risk of death, mainly from asphyxia and soil collapse. The regular occurrence of soil collapses in the artisanal mines may be explained by the fact that artisanal miners do not often conduct prior geological investigations of the sites to test, for example, for soil cohesion and other geological problems, including shrink-swell, corrosiveness, and depth to bedrock.[179] Artisanal miners also dig deeper than the required thirty meters (ninety-eight feet) underground, reaching sometimes 140 meters (460 feet) in tunnels in violation of mining regulations.[180]

Table 3.1. represents the number of reported deaths in artisanal mines in the DRC for the year 2013–2014. The graph indicates that a total of 164 artisanal miners were killed in artisanal mines in five mining regions of the DRC, equivalent to about

3.4 deaths per week. The graph also shows significant gaps in terms of death rates per province. For example, one hundred artisanal miners reportedly died in North Kivu in 2013–2014 while only two artisanal miners were killed in Kasai Oriental within the same time period. It is worth noting that the reporting of the two death cases in Kasai Oriental should not be absolutely interpreted as the real total number of artisanal miner deaths in that province. Many cases of death in artisanal mines caused by soil collapses or other circumstances are commonly not reported to administrative authorities. It is likely that the death rate in the DRC's artisanal mines is much higher than the reported number.

Province	Number of deaths
Katanga	38
Kasai Oriental	2
North Kivu	100
South Kivu	6
Province Oriental	20
Total	**164**

Table 3.1: Number of reported deaths in artisanal mines in the DRC: 2013–2014

Source: Author's calculations based on the UN's Radio Okapi data.

The lack of official and reliable data on death tolls in artisanal mines in the DRC justifies my combined use of questionnaires, NGO reports, and media publications. Roughly 20% of the child miners whom I interviewed in Katanga in 2013, reported that one of their family members or friends was killed in an artisanal mine soil collapse between 2011 and 2013. Reasons for the lack of mortality records may include the remote distance of artisanal mining sites from the urban areas where most public administration offices are located. Indeed, artisanal mining is often conducted in areas where police stations and hospitals are nonexistent, which makes difficult the reporting and recording of death cases. There are also instances where artisanal mining is conducted clandestinely or illegally so that the mine owners, or surviving miners, intentionally refrain from reporting fatal accidents to authorities for fear of eventually being held responsible for potential violations of mining regulations.

One may also wonder as to the percentage of child miner mortality in the DRC as compared to adult miner. There are no official statistics on this issue, either. Nevertheless, research conducted by the World Bank comparing mortality rates for child and adult labor revealed that the occupational mortality rate among children matches the adult occupational mortality rate in all regions of the world.[181] This suggests that children may be working in equally or even more hazardous conditions than adults.[182] In light of this revelation, it is probable that the number of child miners dying in the DRC's artisanal mines may be equal to those of their adult colleagues given that they all execute similar tasks under similarly dangerous conditions.

Injuries and deformities

Child miners are frequently exposed to several kinds of injuries, sometimes so extremely serious that they leave children with permanent lifetime disability and no possibilities of working again in the future.[183] Commonly, cases of injuries in artisanal mines are caused by deep falls into pits, flying rocks or shard, dangerous tools and machinery, or transport of heavy loads.[184] I interviewed some child miners and former child miners who reported to me the different injuries that they had suffered while working in the mines. Tela was one of them. Tela, a former child miner, was nineteen years old when I met him. The particularity of Tela's story is that he was still working in the mines despite that he was walking with a limp. When I saw him, I inquired if I could ask him a couple of questions, which he agreed to without hesitation.

"Could you tell me what happened with your right leg?" I asked.

"One day I was working, here, in this mine and I had an accident," he responded.

"What accident?"

"I was digging for '*mbazi*'[185] at the foot of the hill, and a big stone fell on my right leg and broke it."

"When did it happen?"

"It was four years ago, in 2009."

"What did you do after that?"

"After that, I was taken to the hospital and my leg was put in a cast for some time. But I did not have money to get appropriate medical treatment. I stopped going to the hospital. For that reason, my leg is deformed now."

With artisanal mining, physical disabilities do not only result from untreated injuries. Young child miners regularly use inadequate working postures to both dig for ores underground and crush ores on the surface.[186] They are assigned tasks of lifting and carrying heavy loads of mined minerals for long distances, which may be too weighty for their young skeletal systems.[187] If poor working postures or carrying of heavy loads are executed repetitively; this can lead to skeletal deformations or malformations with some implications for the muscular system.[188] Ultimately, chronic pain, repetitive strain injury and disability can result.[189] Many cases of injuries in artisanal mines are related to tool handling, including shovels, pin bars, and crushing hammers.[190] Table 3.2. represents the results of a survey by medical researchers on the circumstances of accidents in artisanal mines in the DRC's province of Katanga in 2013.[191]

Circumstance of Accidents	Number of accidents by percent
Tools handling	51.5%
Handling heavy loads	32.9%
Falls	11.5%
Asphyxia in underground tunnels	4.1%

Table 3.2: Circumstances of reported accidents in artisanal mines in Katanga

Source: International Journal of Occupational Medicine and Environmental Health

According to the research, out of 392 accidents reported by artisanal miners (adults and children), 51.5% of accidents were due to tools handling, 32.9% were linked to handling of heavy loads (such as bags of ores, sieves of gravel or transportation of bags), 11.5% involved falls, and 4.1% of accidents were caused by asphyxia in underground tunnels.[192]

The large majority of artisanal miners who get injured do not necessarily go to hospitals afterwards to seek appropriate medical care. Most child miners that I interviewed told me that they did not have recourse to medical staff after their accidents. Instead, they were taken care of by peers and families. That lack of involvement by medical staff may perhaps be explained by the fact that hospitals are generally located far from many rural mining sites. Also, access to healthcare services is not free. And, with the situation of extreme poverty in the DRC, it is not surprising for artisanal miners to opt for traditional healers rather than going to modern hospitals which are far more expensive. Only 20% of the DRC's population has access to healthcare, according to a report published by the British-based news agency *The Guardian*.[193]

Illness and insufficient recovery time

Child miners are exposed to dust from digging and crushing ores, toxic substances, dynamite rock blasting, and underground heat.[194] Sometimes, they may have no access to food or clean water in the artisanal mines.[195] Such exposure to chemical materials and contaminated water may lead to serious diseases including respiratory infections, dermatosis, conjunctivitis, diarrhea, and dysentery among others.[196] A study conducted by public health researchers on the toxic ores (including cobalt, copper, uranium, and zinc) exploited by artisanal miners in Katanga concluded that there is a potential link between occupational exposure to these metals, and pathologies such as lung disease, thyroid disorders, and digestive disease.[197] Some of these diseases, particularly respiratory conditions, may be directly related to inhalation of toxic particles released during the mining process.[198] But, it is also possible that many of these health problems are caused by other factors[199] given that most working and non-working children in the DRC face the same difficulties of poor water quality, insufficient immunization, and underdeveloped sanitary systems.[200] Naturally, human bodies also need energy and time to recover in order to combat some of these diseases.[201]

Unfortunately, many child miners are not able to rest when they are ill. During my interviews with medical staff from the rare hospitals located in the vicinity of artisanal mines, I was told that child miners treated for pneumonia or other illness, have recurrent bouts with the same disease condition. One reason that may explain the situation of child miners' re-infection, prolonged illnesses, or sometimes chronic conditions is the lack of sufficient resting time during the disease period to help their bodies to recover.[202]

A lack of proper nutrition may also increase the vulnerability of child miners in contracting infections and other illnesses.[203] A report from the World Bank noted that childhood malnutrition's effects can be lifelong given that its survivors are less physically and intellectually productive and suffer from more chronic illness and disability.[204] Table 3.3. represents the health- and nutrition-related Millennium Development Goals (MDG) indicators for the DRC. The table indicates that chronic malnutrition affects about 38% of children younger than age five in the DRC. The table also shows that the acute malnutrition in the country is 16%, which is higher than the average of 10% in other Sub-Saharan African countries.

	Urban DRC	Rural DRC	DRC	Sub-Saharan Africa
MGD1: Poverty and Hunger				
Prevalence Child Malnutrition (underweight) (% under age 5 years)	22	36	31	30
Prevalence Child Malnutrition (stunting) (% under age 5 years)	29	43	38	41
Prevalence Child Malnutrition (wasting) (% under age 5 years)	12	18	16	10
MDG 4: Child Mortality				
Under-5 Mortality rate (per 1,000 live births)	158	243	220	174
Infant mortality rate (per 1,000 live births)	95	144	128	103
Measles Immunization (% of children ages 12-23 months)	65	40	48	58
MDG 5: Maternal Mortality	---	---	---	
Maternal Mortality Ratio (per 100,000 live births)	---	---	1,289	917
Births Attended by Skilled Health Staff (%)	32	20	24	39
MDG 6: HIV/AIDS, Malaria, and Other Diseases Prevalence of HIV (% Adults aged 15 to 49 prevalence)	---	---	1.1	---
Children aged 0 to 14 Living with HIV			66,000	
Adults aged 15 and older Living with HIV			380,000	
Proportion Sleeping Under Insecticide-Treated Bednets (% children under age 5)	---	---	0.7	2
Proportion of Children with Fever Treated with Anti-Malarials (% children under age 5 with fever)	63	47	52	42
Incidence of Tuberculosis (per 100,000 per year)			384	358
Tuberculosis Cases Detected under DOTS (%)			52	
MDG 7: Environment				
Access to an Improved Water Source (% of population)	84	29	46	58
Access to Improved Sanitation (% of population)	61	39	46	54

Table 3.3: Health and Nutrition-related MDG Indicators, DRC

Source for the HIV/AIDS data: The United Nations Program on HIV/AIDS (UNAIDS).
Source for all other data: World Bank.

HIV/AIDS and Sexually Transmitted Diseases (STDs)

Table 3.3. indicates that the prevalence rate of HIV in the DRC among adults age fifteen- to forty-nine-years old is about 1.1% of the country's population.[205] Even though there are no reliable statistics on the seroprevalence rate among artisanal miner populations in the DRC, the recurrent problems of sexual abuse and prostitution in the mining camps may expose artisanal miners to greater risks of infection with HIV/AIDS and other sexually transmitted diseases (STDs). [206] In the mining camp of Kawama that I visited, artisanal miners (men and women) were living in "promiscuity;" meaning with high level of physical proximity in make-shift structures covered with tarp. Such "promiscuity" combined with the lack of sufficient healthcare services, sanitation/hygiene, and HIV/AIDS awareness can further lead to the propagation of HIV and other STDs among artisanal miners, including girl artisanal miners. [207]

Psychological impacts

"Good mental health implies not only the absence of mental illness and psychiatric disorders, but also balanced self-esteem and sound self-confidence that is, a realistic perception of one's own capacity as well as the ability to analyze constructively and respond adequately to one's surroundings."[208]

In addition to its potential physical harms, mining labor can also have psychological implications for child miners. To assess whether or not mining labor and other worst forms of child labor have psychologically impacted children, it is necessary to evaluate psychological domains[209] including: 1) children's cognitive abilities and cultural competencies;[210] 2) children's personal security, social integration and social competence;[211] and 3) children's personal identity, self-esteem, and self-confidence.[212]

Children's cognitive abilities and cultural competencies

The cognitive abilities and cultural competencies of child workers relate, for example, to their intelligence and communication and technical skills.[213] Researchers have noted that the involvement of children in hazardous work, such as mining, may lead them to eventually resist building their emotional cognitive skills and to become withdrawn, introverted, and uncommunicative.[214] Long working hours, harsh treatment, or deprivation of rest may also breed feelings of frustration and inadequacy for children.[215] Although there are no consistent statistics on the cognitive abilities of child miners in the DRC, a cross-sectional study on children working in construction and welding sectors indicated that a significant portion of these children suffer from psychological immaturity and about 40% of them are affected by abnormal psychological growth.[216]

Children's personal security, social integration and social competence

As for the personal security and social integration, psychologists say that psychological abuse associated with ongoing threats, feelings of fear, fear of not being paid, and witnessing the abuse of others may negatively affect children's self-concept, relationships with others, personal goals, and emotional well-being.[217] In artisanal mining sites, some unaccompanied child miners live away from their families and labor for themselves or non-related adult miners. It may not be unusual for this category of child miners to feel unprotected and scared. Therefore, as a response to those constant feelings of fear and insecurity, many child miners start using drugs regularly.[218] As other researchers have noted, drugs do not constitute a solution to a psychologically stressful situation.[219] Instead, they may lead to additional stress and may ultimately cause mental or emotional disorders.[220]

Children's personal identity, self-esteem and self-confidence

Identity is essential to psychosocial well-being.[221] According to psychologists, children develop their identity throughout different stages of their lives.[222] The experiences of children in developing identity are regularly situated in particular sociocultural contexts, settings and practices, and shaped by their communities or people having authority and influences on their lives.[223]

In Chapter Two, I stated that some children get involved in mining labor because they want to prove their braveness and worth in a society where they are required to work and contribute to the household income. In that sociocultural context, children work to confirm their identity of *mwana-umé* (brave child). For these child miners, working and contributing to the family revenue may constitute a factor that develops confidence, self-esteem and feeling of being valued and respected. During my research, I also interviewed child miners who enthusiastically told me they feel respected and valued when they send a portion of their earnings to their parents and siblings. But, there are also cases where mining labor can work to the detriment of the self-esteem and self-confidence of child miners.[224] For instance, situations related to unpaid/underpaid salary, and employers' humiliation of, manipulation of, and accusation of poor performance can affect the confidence and self-esteem of child laborers.[225] Regarding child mining labor in the DRC, a 2013 report from PACT stated that child miners working alone earn more than their peers working with adults in Katanga.[226] The report also mentioned that younger child miners working for adults may be more vulnerable to exploitation from adults who do not pay them a fair wage.[227] In light of these findings, it is likely that the situation of underpaid and unpaid salaries may have negative effects on the self-esteem and self-confidence of these child miners.

From another perspective, it can also be said that child miners' self-esteem or self-confidence depends on the reactions of those who benefit from child labor.[228] In other words, a child miner's self-esteem is positively developed if the society (family members) recognizes his efforts and contribution to the household revenue.[229] Conversely, the same self-esteem is negatively affected when a child's exploiter (employer) does not notice and appreciate his hard work.[230] The danger is that some may think that child mining labor is acceptable as long as it is appreciated by someone.[231] I disagree with that perception; child mining labor should not be appreciated at all nor should the quality of tasks performed by child miners.[232]

Impacts on education

Mining labor can also have negative educational effects on children, particularly on their school attendance and academic achievement.

Effects on school attendance

A cross-country research conducted by ILO on child labor and education reveals the strong inverse impact of child labor on school attendance rates:[233] the more increasing the level of economic activity of children, the more that school attendance rates decrease.[234] Researchers also note that working children are disadvantaged compared to their non-working counterparts in terms of access to school.[235] Numerous child workers are constrained in their school attendance because of their long working hours or the difficult working conditions of their respective jobs.[236] For instance, in African countries such as Zambia the school attendance of child workers represents about 35% of that of non-working children.[237] In Senegal, the corresponding figure is 60%, and 64% in Mali.[238]

Table 3.4. provides statistics on child labor and education in the DRC. The table indicates that out of 3,327,806 child workers (ages five–fourteen years) in cross-sectors, 67.1% attend school, and 16.2% combine working and attending school. This implies that about 16.7% of child workers do not attend school at all.

Children	Age	Percent / Population
Global Population of Children Out-of-School	-	100% (7,300,000)
Working Children (% and population)	5-14 years	16.9% (3,327,806)
Working Children Attending school (%)	5-14 years	67.1%
Children Combining Work and School (%)	7-14 years	16.2%
Primary School Completion Rate	-	72.8%

Table 3.4: Statistics on Child Labor and Education in the DRC

Source for the Global Population of Children out-of-school: Congo, the Democratic Republic, UNICEF. Source for all other data: US Department of Labor

Some commentators emphasize that the relationship between child labor and education cannot be perceived as evidence of a cause and effect in either direction.[239] This is because "children may be working because they are out of school, rather than out of school because they are working."[240] Therefore, the patterns of causality may vary from one country to another.[241] In the DRC, the significant number of child miners who do not attend school or who combine working and schooling is due to either the nonexistence of educational structures or the lack of free education.[242] No matter what the reasons may be, the working conditions in artisanal mining are incompatible with child school attendance. So, what about child miners' educational achievements?

Effects on education achievements

Mining labor may not only affect children school attendance, but also their academic performance. The above-mentioned ILO report also discloses that the combination of working and attending school can negatively impact child workers' ability to achieve educational success.[243] School directors and teachers that I met with throughout my research consistently told me that the school performances of their working students are lower than those of non-working students. The poor education performance of working children is explained in part by the fact that the time invested by child laborers in working activities decreases their available time for studying and doing homework assignments.[244] Furthermore, child laborers are often physically exhausted by their working activities and less likely to take advantage of their time in the classroom as compared to their non-working counterparts.[245] Poor education performance can also lead to grade repetition, [246] which is likely to discourage child laborers and their families from investing scarce financial resources in paying for education (there is no free public education in the DRC).[247] The combination of these factors increases the probability that a child laborer will drop out of school.[248]

Impacts on child development and prospect of better life

Children's involvement in mining activities has obvious consequences for their development and future. The long working hours prevent children from having a normal childhood,[249] particularly the time for play which may contribute to good cognitive and creative development.[250] Yet poor educational achievements and lack of elementary school attendance can also jeopardize the chance for child miners to have better jobs with higher income in the future. Researchers have noted that, of two individuals with the same background, the one with a better education is more likely to have a higher income.[251] Child miners are probably more likely to earn low incomes and dwell in poverty during their lifetimes than non-working children who finished elementary and secondary school.

As earlier noted, with the hazardous working conditions of artisanal mines, a child miner who gets seriously injured may end up with lifetime disability and no possibilities of working again in the future.[252] This situation may further worsen or perpetuate his precarious living conditions or those of his family. In the current world of competition and modern economy, the formal labor market seeks candidates with more formal skills, including literacy and numeracy.[253] Therefore, education appears to be a condition sine qua non for gaining better employment; and thereby having a better life. Some may still argue that the prospect of a better life for Congolese child miners is unattainable because these children are without either free school or a mechanism to afford education. This argument is valid. In Chapter Five, I further elaborate on actions to be undertaken to address this barrier of child access to education. This includes the necessity for the DRC government (and its partners) to enforce the constitutional provision on free education and build more schools in the remote mining areas so that all children will be equipped with the skills required for getting a better job.

CHAPTER FOUR

Financial Aspects of Child Mining Labor

There is a link between child mining labor in the DRC and the globalized high demand for mined minerals and cheap labor. Child employers, or corporations that source minerals from child miners, pay children less for their mined minerals and demand more of them. This chapter addresses fundamental questions: Who sources from child miners in the DRC? For what quantities? For how much? This implies that to understand the financial aspects of child mining labor, one needs to analyze the supply chain of child minerals; the productivity of child miners; and the profits gained by those who source from child miners.

Supply Chain of Child-Mined Minerals

A supply chain "is an integrated manufacturing process in which raw materials are converted into final products" [254] before being delivered to customers. [255] It directly or indirectly involves all parties in fulfilling the customer request including, but not limited to, raw material suppliers, manufacturers, wholesalers/distributors, retailers, and customers. [256] In the context of mined minerals, the Organization for Economic Co-operation and Development (OECD) Due Diligence Guidance for Responsible Supply Chains of Minerals from Conflict-Affected and High-Risk Areas defines the mineral supply chain as:

> The system of all the activities, organizations, actors, technology, information, resources and services involved in moving the mineral from the extraction site downstream to its incorporation in the final product for end consumers. The process of bringing a raw mineral to the consumer market involves multiple actors and generally includes the extraction, transport, handling, trading, processing, smelting, refining and alloying, manufacturing and sale of end product. [257]

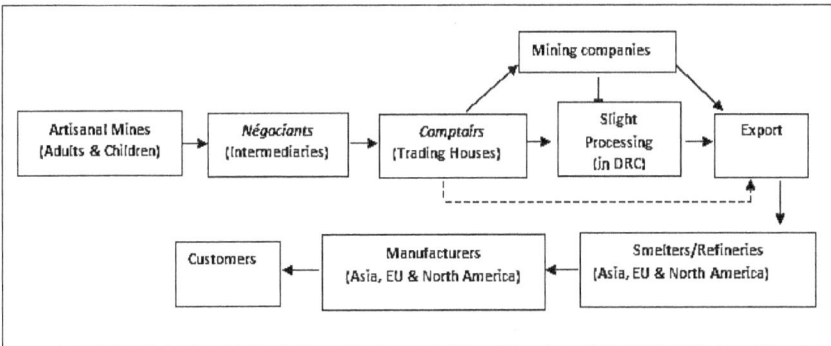

Figure 4.1: Supply Chains of Cobalt Coming from the DRC's Artisanal Mining [238]

Figure 4.1. represents the supply chains of cobalt ores that come from the DRC's artisanal mining sectors. The figure shows that artisanal miners, including child miners, extract raw ores and sell them to *négociants*. [258] The *négociants* resell the minerals to trading houses (*comptoirs*); and the trading houses supply mining companies with cobalt ores. [259] The *comptoirs* and the mining companies may either slightly process the raw ores or export them directly to smelters and refineries in Asia, the European Union, or North America (Canada and the United States) for further refining and transformation.[260] The figure also indicates that after transformation, the refined cobalt products are then sold to manufacturers for different usages; and from there, sold to consumers as finished products.[261] This means, before reaching customers at the end of the chain, the supply chain of artisanal mined minerals commonly involves: artisanal miners, intermediaries (négociants and trading houses), mining companies, smelters/refineries, and manufacturers.

Artisanal miners

Artisanal miners are some of the biggest suppliers of mined minerals, contributing to about 90% of all mineral production of the DRC.[262] In the DRC, artisanal miners may be organized in an association called the "cooperative of artisanal miners." According to Articles 234 to 237 of the DRC Mining Regulations, miners who hold valid artisanal mining cards have a right to form mining cooperatives, which entitle them to freely obtain from local authorities artisanal mining zones (*zone d'exploitation artisanale*) to conduct their mining activities.[263] By the laws, artisanal miners can only extract and sell their ores to mine traders rather than exporting them outside of the country.

It is not uncommon for many artisanal miner cooperatives to have (un)written exclusive supply agreements with particular *négociants* (mine traders), *comptoirs* (trading houses), or mining companies.[264] Numerous artisanal miner cooperatives are financed or sponsored by trading houses and mining companies and are required to exclusively sell their raw ores to their sponsors.[265] However, artisanal miners are also free to join any cooperative of their choice. Many artisanal miners that I interviewed did not adhere to cooperatives; they worked independently. They are free to sell their raw ores to any mining traders.

Négociants and trading houses

The *négociants* are local mine traders who are authorized to buy and sell mined minerals from artisanal miners. The DRC Mining Code stipulates that the function of *négociants* is exclusively reserved for Congolese nationals.[266] *Négociants* are required to hold valid trader's cards (*carte de négociant*) issued by the provincial authorities.[267] Figure 4.1. also shows that the *négociants* are generally those who supply the mine trading houses with mined minerals. Article 1(10) of the Mining Code defines the authorized trading houses (*comptoirs agréés*) as "any (juristic) person authorized to purchase mineral substances extracted by artisanal mining methods from traders or artisanal miners, for the purpose of reselling them locally or exporting them in accordance with the provisions of the Mining Code." It appears that unlike the *négociants*, the mine trading houses can purchase, sell, and export mined minerals. In terms of the Mining Code, both Congolese and foreign nationals are eligible to own trading houses.[268] The law requires foreign traders to hold valid foreign work permits to reside and travel within the mining zones.[269] Yet, most of the trading houses that I visited in Katanga were principally owned by non-Congolese nationals, particularly those from Asia.

Mining companies, smelters, and refineries

Many mining companies purchase ores from artisanal miners to supply their production.[270] However, not all mining companies operating in the DRC buy minerals that originate from artisanal mining. There are some mining companies in the DRC that own mines and quarries, in which they exploit minerals, process, and export them. Prior to 2013, many mining companies in the DRC, particularly private companies, would export raw cobalt and copper ores from the country without processing them. With the adoption of the 2013 Ministerial Decrees[271] on the regulation of exportation of merchant products, the national government banned the exportation of all concentrated mineral products from the country without prior processing.[272] These decrees were just a replication and extension of a previous provincial decree adopted in Katanga in 2010, which was motivated by the need to force the mining operators to build metallurgic factories in the DRC to produce raw ores locally.[273] Despite those decisions, there are still almost no cutting-edge metallurgic factories in the DRC that can fully transform raw cobalt, copper and other ores. To build more modern metallurgic factories would require sufficient energy for the efficient functioning of machineries, but there is a recurrent energy deficit in the DRC[274] so that local mining companies still continue to export their ores outside of the country for further refining and transformation. The existing metallurgic factories in the DRC are only able to slightly refine raw minerals to some modest level or grade.[275] Tables 4.1, 4.2, 4.3. and 4.4. (*see*: Appendix B) provide the lists of smelters and distributors of refined cobalt, tantalum (derived from coltan), and tin. The tables indicate that most of largest smelters and distributors of refined cobalt, tantalum, and tin ores are principally located in Asia, the European Union and the United States.

It is worth noting that the smelters listed in the Appendix B do not necessarily source their minerals from the DRC. Even if they do source from the DRC and its artisanal mines, there is no substantial evidence that the raw minerals originating from the DRC were actually mined by children. The complex question of traceability of children's minerals will be addressed further. In the meantime, it is obvious that child miners in the DRC and elsewhere do not have depots to store indefinitely their products. Soon after their extraction, child-labored minerals are purchased by intermediaries and mine traders who resell them to mining companies and smelters for processing outside of the country.

At the refineries, raw ores can be purified and transformed into powdery products or different metallic particles depending on the type of minerals and the applications intended for them.[276] For example, Figure 4.2. shows the flowsheet of cobalt process conducted by the DRC's state-owned company Gécamines. The figure illustrates that the transformation of cobalt ores (or other ores) may be a long process conducted through different stages, during which the raw ores can also be mixed with other chemical substances and metals in order to obtain refined products.[277]

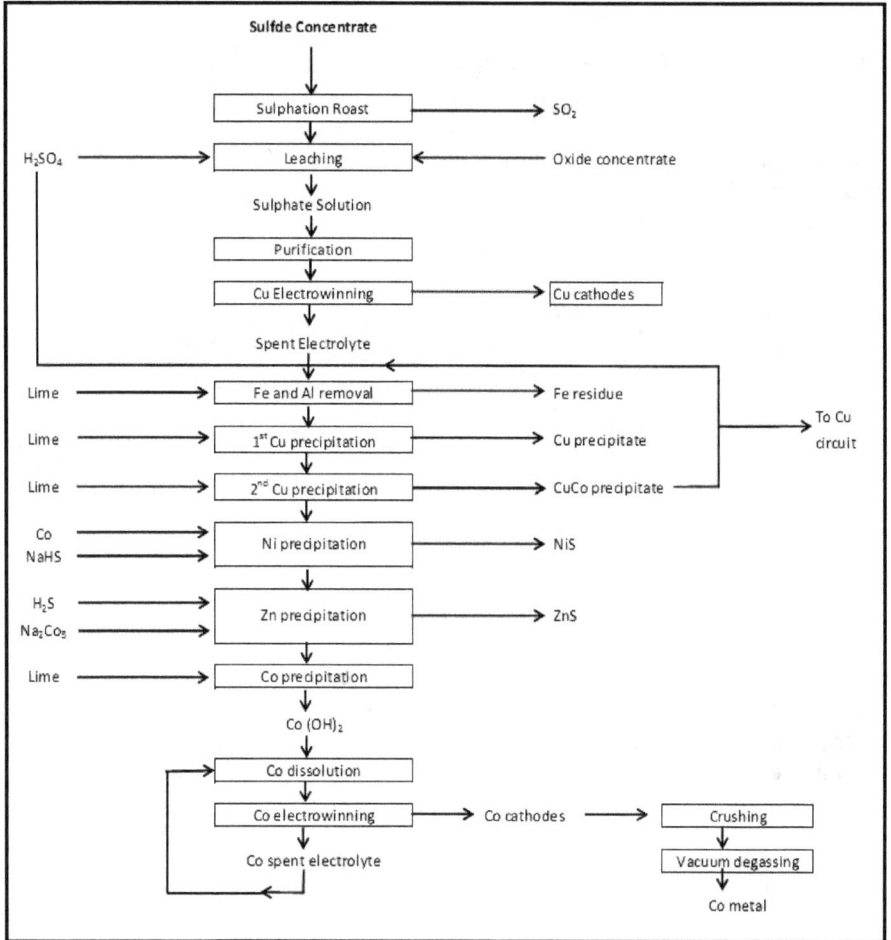

table 4.2: Flowsheet of Cobalt Process by Gecamines
Source: Cobalt Development Institute

Table 4.5. indicates that refined cobalt ores may be used as catalysts in petrochemical industries for the process of making biofuel, or as super alloys for jet turbines, or as fundamental components for rechargeable batteries for numerous types of electronic devices including cell phones, computers, tablets, hybrid electric vehicles, and others. Likewise, Table 4.6. shows another of the DRC's key minerals, coltan ore (*see*: Appendix C). Coltan is an abbreviation for columbite-tantalite, and is used in the fabrication of electronics. Tantalum metal is extracted from coltan and is used for electronic circuits in cell phones and computer hard drive discs.

Market Sector	Usages
Petrochemicals	Catalysts for biofuel
Super Alloys	Jet turbines and gas turbine generators
Electronics	Rechargeable batteries for cell phones, computers, tablets, hybrid electric cars and others.
Carbides and Diamond Tools	Stainless and heat-resisting High-strength low-alloy Magnets & high speed steel
Ceramic	Colorizer in paint, porcelain, glass, pottery and enamels.
Other	Radioactive cobalt-60 for cancer treatment

Table 4.5: Industry Consumption and Usage of Cobalt
Source: U.S. Geological Survey

Manufacturers

Tables 4.5. and 4.6. indicate that refined ores such as cobalt and coltan have numerous uses in numerous industries. Manufacturers of cell phones, computers, televisions, DVD players, videogames and other electronic devices are among the largest consumers of cobalt, tantalum, and tin. For instance, according to the Cobalt Development Institute, about 38% of the world production of cobalt ores is used to produce batteries for electronic and automotive devices.[278] Other markets that use cobalt include super alloys (17%), carbides and diamond tools (10%), petrochemical products (8%) and others (27%).[279] Many electronics manufacturers consume cobalt, tantalum, or other ores source products partially or totally from the smelters listed in Tables 4.2, 4.3, and 4.4. (*see*: Appendix B).

Traceability of Minerals

The traceability of minerals is a mechanism that exists to ensure that the origin of the minerals that are exported is beyond doubt.[280] This mechanism is pivotal for the mineral certification systems intended to encourage responsible trade of clean minerals rather than trading of tainted minerals.[281] The term "tainted minerals," as opposed to clean minerals, refers to mined minerals linked to either human rights abuses (such as child labor) or conflict.[282] Conflict minerals are ores or their derivatives that are exploited to directly or indirectly finance or benefit armed groups in the DRC.[283]

In Chapter One, it is noted that the DRC experienced a deadly armed conflict from the late 1990s to the early 2000s. The UN Panel of Experts also established the link between the DRC's conflict and the illegal exploitation of minerals in the country.[284] In 2010, the US Congress voted to approve Section 1502 of the Dodd-

Frank Law (also known as the Conflict Minerals Law), which requires American companies to disclose to the Securities and Exchange Commission (SEC) whether their products contain conflict minerals or human rights violation minerals originating from the DRC, particularly tin, tantalum, tungsten and gold ores.[285] US multinational companies are legally required to set up and implement their own traceability systems to record the movement of minerals from the pits where they were extracted to the cross-border refineries where they were transformed.[286] That traceability system is supposed to be regularly audited by a credible third party to certify if the mines from which the minerals originated were free from any presence of rebel groups or soldiers; or if belligerents were directly or indirectly benefiting from the mineral trade through illegal tax collection at any point of the mineral trading operation.[287] Likewise, the 2011 OECD Due Diligence Guidance for Responsible Supply Chains of Minerals from Conflict-Affected and High-Risk Areas (Guidance) sets up rules on the transparency of the supply chains of tin, tantalum, tungsten and gold ores. The Guidance provides a detailed framework for companies to respect human rights, avoid contributing to conflict through their mineral sourcing practices, and enable source countries to benefit from their mineral resources.[288]

Nevertheless, the tracing of the supply chains of tainted minerals from mine origins to smelters can be a lengthy and complex process for manufacturers; it can also present practical challenges. Indeed, the raw ores produced, for instance, by children in the DRC's artisanal mines are commonly not recorded and reported even in the non-conflict zones under the control of the legitimate government.[289] And, prior to their export and transformation outside of the country, these child-labor minerals are mingled with other minerals produced from other sources, such as adult artisanal miners and industrial mining companies.[290] This bundling of minerals from different production sources can make it almost impossible to disaggregate the minerals produced by child labor from the rest.[291] Many of the local mine traders I interviewed told me that they do not put into separate bags the cobalt ores purchased from adult artisanal miners and those from child miners. Furthermore, the same difficulty of identifying the mines of origin and their actual miners can equally be observed with conflict minerals which are often smuggled out of the DRC via neighboring countries before being exported to smelters and refineries.[292]

Another practical challenge for manufacturers in tracking the real origin of the refined metals used in their products is due to the fact that that raw ores are often transformed. At the refineries, raw ores such as cobalt and coltan are transformed into heat resistant powders.[293] For example, tantalum powder extracted from coltan is used to create the capacitors that manufacturers purchase to use for the circuit boards of their electronic products.[294] From the manufacturer's perspective, it may appear difficult to look at a capacitor X and determine its association with child labor or armed conflicts. This is because the capacitor X may have been produced with coltan compiled from different sources (including those connected with human rights abuses) and mixed with other chemical substances at different stages of refining, all of which may deteriorate the "mineral fingerprint" of the original raw ores. Researchers from Germany have investigated "fingerprinting" conflict mineral coltan by analyzing the elemental coltan concentrates via WD-X-ray fluorescence and X-ray diffraction to establish "the composition and amounts of trace elements presence in the sample."[295] This technique could potentially work for the analysis of both pure coltan ore and mixed source coltan.[296] Even though this scientific technique may make possible the identification of ores emanating from mines associated with armed conflicts or child labor, the process may be expensive and lengthy for manufacturers.

In light of the complexity of identifying of the origin of minerals extracted from mines violating human rights, a group of electronics companies created the Electronic Industry Citizenship Coalition (EICC) to improve the transparency and traceability of metals in their supply chain.[297] The EICC's approach on mineral traceability consists of three stages:

1) Conflict-free smelter initiative which consists of identifying smelters who can demonstrate after a third party audit assessment that the raw ores they refine did not come from sources that contribute to conflict in the DRC.[298] Tables 4.3. and 4.4. (*see*: Appendix B) catalogue the conflict-free smelters for coltan and tin ores who comply with the assessment protocols, and from whom electronics companies can source from. However, not all coltan or tin smelters operate in compliance with the conflict-free assessment protocols nor do all electronics manufacturers necessarily source from smelters complying with the conflict-free assessment protocols.

2) Tracing of ores back to the smelters and mine of origin.[299] Most smelters involved in conflict-free smelter initiative are required to use a standardized reporting template to provide information regarding mineral country of origin and the local smelters and refiners utilized to transform the raw materials. Table 4.7. represents the Conflict Minerals Reporting Template (*see*: Appendix D), which is divided into two main parts: company information and a list of questions. The questions deal with the type of ores, their origins, the smelters, the company internal policy on conflict minerals, and so on. It is worth noting that the reporting template does not contain any explicit question relating to child labor in the mines where the ores were extracted. Some may say that the lack of explicit mention of child labor or other forms of human rights abuses is because the template concerns primarily the reporting of conflict minerals. Even if this response might be pertinent, the danger of the absence of an unequivocal question on child labor may lead companies and smelters to constantly overlook the recurrent problem of child mining labor. Considering that the scope of the Dodd-Frank Law provisions and the OECD Guidance cover both conflict minerals and human rights issues in mineral supply chains; it seems logical to have some explicit questions on child mining labor in the Conflict Minerals Reporting Template.

3) Bagging and Tagging Minerals.[300] The OECD Guidance also requires that ores originating from the DRC be stored and transported in bags having official tags confirming each consignment's origin, weight and composition; these tags convey the shipments to the smelters that refine the ore into metal.[301] This requirement has been currently implemented in Katanga to trace untainted minerals (particularly coltan, tin, and tungsten) from the mines to the smelters. The problem with this system relates to the

stage of the supply chains when the minerals are effectively bagged and tagged. Indeed, during my research in the field, I discovered that many minerals in Katanga are only bagged and tagged with official seals when they reach the mine trading houses. In other words, before reaching the mine trading houses (meaning at the artisanal mines and *négociants* levels), the minerals are not really monitored. With such a lack of official tagging at the early stage of the supply chains, it is possible that some minerals bagged and tagged and exported as conflict-free or child-labor-free may have been, in fact, mixed with child labor/conflict products before reaching the trading houses. Therefore, for the efficiency of the system, it is imperative that minerals should be bagged and tagged with official seals at the artisanal mines where they are first extracted. Perhaps the bagging and tagging of minerals starts at the trading house level because it is easier to control the movement of minerals at this stage: there is a plethoric number of artisanal mines compared to trading houses. Also, it may be financially constraining to print bags and tags with official stamps for all the artisanal mines that exist in the DRC. Regardless what the reasons may be, the bagging and tagging of minerals should begin from the pits for a more effective traceability system.

No matter their complexity, the burden of tracing mineral supply chains falls upon the companies. Companies have a responsibility to ensure that the raw materials used in their products do not originate from mines that are linked to armed conflicts or human rights violations such as child labor. The question posed is what sanctions are applied to the companies that "negligently" fail to comply with their obligations under the Dodd-Frank Law?

Legal Consequences for the Failure of Mineral Tracking and Reporting Requirements

Neither the 2010 Section 1502 of the Dodd-Frank Law nor the 2012 SEC's regulations for Disclosing Use of Conflict Minerals set up explicit sanctions against US companies for failure to trace and report their use of conflict minerals. This silence of the conflict mineral provisions on penalties for the breach of reporting requirements may create a kind of "juridical insecurity" to the extent that it may seem to weaken the deterrent effects of conflict mineral laws that prevent potential offenders from violating the law. However, as an implementing agency of Section 1502 of the Dodd-Frank Law, the SEC can bring civil actions in federal court or administrative proceedings before an administrative law judge against companies that violate Section 1502 of the Dodd-Frank Law and SEC's regulations.[302] For example in approaching the civil court, the SEC may seek an injunction from the court requiring companies to audit their supply chains or describe conflict materials in their products. [303] Additionally, the SEC can seek civil monetary penalties, [304] with the amount to be determined by the court.

Nevertheless, on July 8, 2014, the US government adopted Executive Order 13671, which contained sanctions relating to conflict minerals in the supply chain of companies.[305] The Executive Order did not impose a new public reporting requirement on companies to disclose their use of conflict minerals in their supply chains. But it authorized the Office of Foreign Asset Control (OFAC) to impose sanctions against:

> Any person to be responsible for or complicit in, or to have engaged in, directly or indirectly in actions or policies that threaten the peace, security, or stability of the DRC[306]... and...support to persons, including armed groups, involved in activities that threaten the peace, security, or stability of the DRC or that undermine democratic processes or institutions in the DRC, through the illicit trade in natural resources of the DRC.[307]

The term "person" includes both natural persons, and juristic persons such as private companies. There is no definition of the concept "natural resources" in the OFAC laws and regulations on the DRC sanctions program;[308] natural resources may comprise substances such as minerals, forests and others. Unlike the SEC regulations for Disclosing Use of Conflict Minerals, the OFAC Laws and Regulations on the DRC Sanctions Program explicitly set up monetary and criminal penalties for the violations of the Executive Order 13413. The civil monetary penalties can be imposed up to $250,000 or twice the amount of the underlying transaction against any person who violates, attempts to violate, conspires to violate, or causes a violation of the Executive Order or regulations.[309] Upon the conviction of the offenders, criminal penalties of up to $1,000,000, imprisonment for up to 20 years, or both can be imposed.[310] The offenders of the Executive Order can also be subjected to additional penalties under the UNPA (United Nations Participation Act) of up to $1,000,000, imprisonment for up to 20 years or both.[311] The Executive Order 13671 appears to be a sort of "supplement" of Section 1502 of the Dodd-Frank Law in the way that companies purchasing conflict minerals from the DRC may also fall under the scope of its coverage, and be punished accordingly.[312]

The 2016 US Government Accountability Office Report to Congressional Committees on SEC Conflict Minerals Rule noted that about 2,500 companies filed the conflict minerals disclosures between 2014 and 2015.[313] Out of the 1,321 companies that filed the reports in 2014: 67% of them were unable to determine if the minerals in their products originated from the DRC or adjoining countries;[314] 4% declared that their products contained minerals coming from the DRC or adjoining countries; 24% did not use minerals coming from the DRC or adjoining countries; 2% disclosed that their materials utilized in their products emanated from scrap or recycled sources; and 3% made no declaration on the origin of minerals in their products.[315]

Numerous companies who reported to the SEC in 2014 submitted their reports late, after the reporting deadline of May 31, 2014.[316] This is because the National Association of Manufacturers (NAM) approached the U.S. Court of Appeals for the District of Columbia, in September 2013, to challenge the 2012 SEC final rule on Disclosing Use of Conflict Minerals (see: Appendix E: NAM vs. SEC case).[317]

Child Mining Labor Productivity and Profits from Child Minerals

In analyzing child mining labor in the DRC, it is important to assess how the productivity of child workers factors into the profits made by the mine traders who employ or source from them.

Child mining labor productivity

Economists describe "labor productivity" as the output to the labor hours used in the production of that output[318] or the ratio of a volume measure of output to a volume measure of input use.[319] In the context of child mining, child labor productivity may refer to the ratio of the quantity of mined minerals produced by child miners (during a certain period of time) to the quantity of time used to produce these minerals. The measurement of the daily productivity of a child miner may consist of dividing the quantity of mined minerals produced by a child miner per day by the number of hours he/she spent to produce these minerals.[320]

One may wonder as to the importance of determining the productivity of child miners. A knowledge of child mining productivity is important because not only it does help in appraising the scope of child labor-tainted materials commercialized at both global and local markets, but it can also help to persuade those who unethically source from child miners to change their policies.[321]

There are several challenges in evaluating child miner labor productivity. As noted above, child miners in the DRC contribute in the production of several types of minerals, including cobalt, coltan, diamond, gold and others. The problem is that the real quantity of minerals produced by those child miners in the DRC is unknown due to a lack of official and reliable data.[322] Minerals produced by child miners are not recorded and are commonly mixed with raw ores coming from different sources of production.[323] This makes it difficult to differentiate the quantity of minerals produced by children from those produced by adult artisanal miners and industrial mining companies.[324] Table 4.8. represents an estimate of labor productivity of child miners in the cobalt artisanal mines in Katanga. To calculate approximately the quantity of cobalt ores produced by child miners in the DRC, I used a simple method of estimation based on economic assumptions and available data on overall cobalt production in the DRC.[325]

Facts
The World Production of cobalt in 2012 was estimated at 110,000 tons (t).
Out of 110,000 t, 60,000 t were produced by the DRC alone (including both industrially and artisanally mined minerals)

About 75% of all DRC's cobalt production comes from artisanal mining (approximately 45,000t).
Between 100,000 to 150,000 people work in the cobalt artisanal mines in the DRC, of which 40,000 to 50,000 are children.

General Assumption
There were 45,000 child miners working in 2012 in the DRC's cobalt artisanal mines (performing different tasks, such as digging, washing, sifting or transportation of minerals). All 45,000 child miners were working everyday throughout the year 2012.

Each child miner produced 0.5 kilogram (kg) of cobalt per day.

Unit Assumptions		Monthly Production	Annual Production
Production	**Unit Quantity (kg)**		
Cobalt production per child miner	0.5k per child miner per day	**15kg**	**182.5kg**
Total Production (for all child miners)		**22,500kg**	**8,212,500kg (8,212.5 tons)**

Table 4.8: Child Cobalt Productivity in Katanga, DRC (2012)
Source: Author's Calculations.

Table 4.8. indicates that one child in the DRC's artisanal mines produces at least 182.5 kilogram (kg) of cobalt per year. This number comes from the general assumption that each child miner in the DRC produces daily a quantity of 0.5 kg of cobalt, which is multiplied by 365 days to estimate the annual production of each child miner. I chose "0.5kg of cobalt per day per child miner" as a minimal amount to enable me to estimate the productivity of child miners in the cobalt artisanal mines. In reality, all of the child miners that I met during my field research in cobalt artisanal mines in Katanga produced far more than 0.5kg of cobalt per day. Most child miners work almost every day for more than ten hours per day and the cobalt ores are relatively close to the surface; these factors make larger amounts likely. In the same way, children whose tasks consist of sifting and washing ores can also sift and wash more than 0.5kg of cobalt during the same timeframe.

Based on the same assumptions, the table also indicates all child miners involved in cobalt artisanal mining in the DRC produced about 8,212,500kg of cobalt (corresponding to 8,212.5 tons) in 2012.[326] Indeed, 8,212.5 tons of cobalt represents approximately 14% of the DRC's total production of cobalt in 2012 (estimated at 60,000 tons) and 7.5% of the world total production of cobalt in 2012 (estimated 110,000 tons).[327] From these calculations, it appears that child miners contribute enormously to cobalt production in the DRC; and that there is a significant quantity of cobalt tainted with child labor, which is sold at both international and local markets.

Profits from Child Minerals

In Chapter Two, I noted that employers and buyers have a financial incentive to hire child miners or source minerals from them. Unlike adult artisanal miners, child miners are less knowledgeable of the market value of their products and are not skilled at negotiating their wages and shares of minerals. [328] Table 4.9. provides an estimation of profit that a *négociant* of cobalt in Katanga who sources from child miners may gain. A *négociant* is a local mine trader who buys raw ores directly from artisanal miners and sells the minerals to the mine trading houses (*comptoirs*). Some *négociants* also hire artisanal miners to work on their behalf.

General Assumption
There are 15 child miners who work for a *négociant* (mine trader).
Mine Trader supplies all 15 child miners with tools to dig for cobalt.
Each child miner produces 75 kg of cobalt per month and receives a flat salary of
$1 per day.
Mining activity is conducted twelve months per year
Wholesale price of cobalt at the local trading houses is $1.32 per kg.

Unit Assumptions		Monthly Profit & Loss	
Revenues	Unit Price($)	Monthly Revenues	
Cobalt wholesale	$1.32		$1,485
Operating Costs		Operating Expenses	
Child Miner Wage	$1 per child miner per day		$450
Accountant/Foreman	$1.75 per day		$52.5
Taxes (Card of Négociant Category B)	$150 per year (or $12.5 per month)		$12.5
Transportation	$150 per month		$150
Utilities, repairs & miscellaneous	$0.10 per child miner per day		$45
		Total Operating Expenses	$710
Fixed Cost		Gross Profit	$775
Tools & Other Equipment	$250	%Gross Margin	52%
		Depreciation (Tools & other Equipment)	$7
		Net Profit	$768
		% of Net Profit	52%
		Annual Revenues	$17,820
		Annual Net Profit	$9,216
		per child miner	$614

Table 4.9: Estimation of Profit Gained by Local Cobalt Trader Sourcing from Child Miners in Katanga
Source: Author's Calculations.

Based on the assumptions and calculations from Table 4.9, a *négociant* who employs fifteen child miners can make annual revenues of about $18,000 and net profit of $9,200 after deduction of operating costs, taxes and depreciation. The percentage of the net profit is 52%, representing the ratio of the amount of net profit and the amount of total revenues. It is important to mention that operating costs for a *négociant* employing child miners are very minimal. The average earnings or wages of children working in cobalt artisanal mines in Katanga are estimated somewhere between $0.75 and $3 per day, which is low compared to amount of effort that child miners put in to produce ores. And, *négociants* do not usually incur expenses for sheltering their child "employees." Many child miners, whose family houses are far away from the mining sites, sleep in the mining depots or mining camps nearby the mining sites where they work. Those who live in the vicinity of the mines, return to their family houses at the end of the working day. Furthermore, the cost of transportation of raw ores from the mines to the trading houses is cheap to the extent that there many trading houses are located near the artisanal mining sites; the proximity of mining sites and mine trading houses reduces the cost of transportation of minerals. In addition, *négociants* are not subjected to higher taxes in exercising their activities. The Mining Code only requires *négociants* to possess *négociant* cards that are valid for one year. As of 2013, a *négociant* card for category B *négociants* (those purchasing cobalt directly from artisanal mines) cost about $150 while the *négociant* card for category A *négociants* (those operating into commercial centers) was $500.[329]

Table 4.10. represents an estimation of profit gained by the mine trading houses that export child labor cobalt. The table shows that owners of mine trading houses make annual revenues of several millions of dollars for sourcing from child miners and reselling their products on the global market.

General Assumption

There are 20 *négociants* (mine traders) who each supply the owner of the mine trading house with 1,125kg of raw cobalt per month.

Each *négociant* employs 15 children to supply the *négociant*'s monthly quota of minerals.

Wholesale price of cobalt at the trading houses is $1.32 per kg.

Owner of the trading house processes cobalt ores at local refinery before exporting them.

Owner of trading house employs 7 people to assist with ores storing, accounting and other tasks.

Owner of the trading house resells cobalt ores at the global market.

Wholesale price of cobalt at the global market $31.6 per kg.

Unit Assumptions		Monthly Profit & Loss	
Revenues	**Unit Price($)**		**Monthly**
		Revenues	
Cobalt Wholesale at Global Market	$31.6 per kg[330]		**$711,000**
Price of Goods			
Cobalt Wholesale at Local Market	$1.32 per kg		**$29,000**
Operating Costs		**Operating Expenses**	
Employee Wage	$250 per employee per month		$1,750
Rent and utilities	$2,500 per month		$2,500
Refinery	$5 per kg per month		$ 112,500
Transportation/Export	$10 per kg per month		$ 225,000
		Total Operating Expenses	**$ 341,750**
Fixed Cost		**Gross Profit**	**$340,250**
Tools & Other Equipment	$5,000	%Gross Margin	48%
		Taxes	
		Annual tax	$5,000
		Exportation tax (1% of value of the exported ores)[331]	$7,110
		Total Taxes	**$12,110**
		Depreciation of tools & other Equipment	**$83**
		Net Profit	**$328,057**
		% of Net Profit	46%
		Annual Revenues	**$8,532,000**
		Annual Net Profit	**$3,936,684**
		per child miner	$13,122

Table 4.10: Estimation of Profit Gained by Owner of Trading Houses Exporting Child Labor Cobalt
Source: Author's Calculations.

As these calculations show, child mining labor is sadly a highly profitable business. This is particularly true for those who source from children: their expenses are very low and their profits are extremely high. As for the child miners, they work in dangerous conditions and routinely expose themselves to the risks of fatal accidents for meager revenues.

CHAPTER FIVE

Corporate Social Responsibility and Child Mining Labor

During the last two decades, there has been growing global concern in many commercial sectors, including the mining industry, on the importance of corporate social responsibility (CSR).[332] There has been a perception that companies should not only answer to their owners and shareholders, but also to other stakeholders, such as the community at large.[333] Therefore, companies are now required to take responsibility for water pollution, working conditions, child labor in their supply chains, or social development of the local population where they conduct business. However, the issue of CSR has often been overlooked in regards to developing countries, including the DRC, where there is habitually dysfunctional governance.[334] In fact, many companies operating in the developing world commonly take advantage of weak governance to escape from their responsibilities vis-à-vis local communities. As previously noted in Chapter Four, most minerals produced by child miners in the DRC end up in the hands of mining companies/manufacturers after transiting through traders or smelters. In sourcing minerals directly or indirectly from child miners, companies are able to lower their labor costs, make high profits, and maximize returns for their shareholders.[335] In light of their financial powers coupled with their social responsibilities, a fundamental question is: In what ways can corporations help to combat the social scourge of child labor in the DRC's mining industry? Before answering this question, it is important to understand what corporate social responsibility is.

Understanding the Concept of Corporate Social Responsibility

There is not a universally accepted definition of CSR.[336] Some of the more comprehensive and recent definitions come from the World Business Council for Sustainable Development (WBCSD) and the European Commission. According to the WBCSD, CSR is described as: "The continuing commitment by business to behave ethically and contribute to economic development while improving the quality of life of the workforce and their families as well as of the local community and society at large."[337] Likewise, the European Commission defines CSR as: "The responsibility of enterprises for their impacts on society....Enterprises should have in place a process to integrate social, environmental, ethical human rights and consumer concerns into their business operations and core strategy in close collaboration with their stakeholders."[338]

In short, CSR refers to an industry practice that involves companies' participation in initiatives that benefit local populations in places where they conduct their business.[339] In the context of mining exploitation in the DRC, the Congolese Mining Code and Mining Regulations also have some provisions dealing with the social responsibility of mining companies. Even though those provisions do not explicitly mention and define the term "social responsibility," they require companies investing in the mining sector to initiate and implement CSR projects. For instance, Article 69(2)(g) of the Mining Code compels investors applying for a mine exploitation license to submit a plan as to how the (mining) project will contribute to the development of the local community. Additionally, Article 451 of the Mining Regulations emphasizes that the applicant should conduct an Environmental Impact Assessment (EIA) to assess how the mining exploitation would affect the local community. In conducting the EIA, the applicant should also "consult and involve local populations, and undertake measures such as…informing local populations on the positive and negative impacts of the potential mining exploitation; determining initiatives to rehabilitate and mitigate the impacts of mining exploitation; and compensating those affected by the mining exploitation."[340]

The DRC's mining laws list some attributes of CSR without defining the concept itself. The attributes of CSR include, for instance, the implementation of programs for the development of the local community, and the compensation of populations to be affected by mining activities. But there are some loopholes in the DRC legal framework on the CSR of mining companies. One of the gaps is that the legislation in the DRC is silent about the nature of initiatives to be implemented by the companies, the timeframe of the implementation of the development programs, the scope and procedure of compensations for affected populations, and the potential sanctions in the case of a company's failure to comply with its social obligations. This silence in the mining provisions can imply that social responsibility is not a mandatory requirement or legally binding commitment for mining companies in the DRC.[341] Instead, it is merely a voluntary commitment that mining companies can take towards local communities and whose implementation is based on the good faith of the companies.[342] The civil society in the DRC is the entity that is most critical of the provisions dealing with CSR. Leaders in the civil society observe that many mining companies operating in the DRC fail to execute the development plans for local communities that they submitted during their request for exploitation licenses.[343] In addition, companies do not invest enough in CSR activities after they begin their mining operations.[344] For instance, research on the CSR practices of Chinese mining companies in the DRC's Katanga province, conducted by a Congolese NGO called ACIDH (*Action Contre l'Impunité pour les Droits de l'Homme*), revealed that many private Chinese companies use child labor and do not contribute to economic development and improvement of the quality of life in the local communities.[345] At their installation, these companies had promised the local populations that they would provide them with clean water and electricity, and would build schools and hospitals.[346] But after years of mining exploitation, they have done nothing for these communities.[347] Yet, the private Chinese mining companies operating in the DRC are not the only companies that fail to comply with their obligations to the local communities. There are also some Western mining companies that do not invest in CSR programs in the DRC. In 2012, British journalists investigated mining exploitation in the DRC's Katanga province disclosed that the Swiss-based company Glencore was involved in cases of environmental damage (pollution of water with acid),[348] child labor,[349] and tax invasion, which inhibit the economic development of local communities.[350]

During my field research in Katanga, I visited mining areas located where Chinese and/or Western companies operate. I observed that those mining areas lacked basic infrastructure such as asphalt roads. The local populations living in those areas did not have access to potable water, electricity, adequate healthcare service, or schools for their children. Local NGO representatives whom I interviewed on this issue informed me that, in reality, only a few companies actualize their CSR programs. Most companies do not implement their CSR activities or they perform some minor programs more for corporate publicity than for resolving the real needs of the local populations. As an illustration, one of the NGO representatives explained to me that:

> There is a mining company that has recently built a small market where local people can come to buy or sell agricultural products, food, and other items. It took almost five years for the market to be officially opened. In the meantime, there is a shortage of schools and hospitals in the very same locality where that market was built.

This means that, for that NGO member, some companies do not prioritize their CSR activities based on the needs of the local communities. Building a marketplace would not seem to be a priority for a community that lacks access to potable water or electricity. As a result, local populations perceive the mining companies as "rough capitalists"[351] who exploit their natural resources without a real willingness to invest in social development programs.

In response, a coalition of civil society members in Katanga has recently called for an amendment of the provisions of the Mining Code relating to the social responsibility of the mining companies.[352] The coalition has proposed the incorporation of stipulations clearly defining the social responsibility of mining companies; making compulsory the company's contributions to local community development; setting specific criteria to assess the company's social performance; and establishing sanctions against companies for their failure to comply with their social obligations.[353] As of January 2015, the national parliament had not yet amended the existing mining law to incorporate these civil society recommendations. The adoption of a more comprehensive and binding provision on CSR at the national level could be very advantageous to local communities across the country to the extent that it would establish a minimal list of key CSR projects to be implemented, and the timeframe of their execution for all mining companies. Indeed, NGO workers that I interviewed told me that almost all communities located in mining regions in the DRC experience the same challenges of inaccessibility to basic infrastructures, but at different scales. From the catalogue of CSR activities set by the new law, companies would prioritize their initiatives based on the specific needs and desires of the local communities. Consequently, at the end, all local communities in different mining regions in the DRC would have access to identical infrastructures.[354] In that case, the social responsibility of the mining companies would be considered as "standard practice" for all companies.[355] However, even if such a law containing stipulations on CSR initiatives were adopted in the DRC, there is no absolute guarantee that it would be efficiently implemented in practice. In a country like the DRC where the implementation of laws is commonly weak due to corruption and mismanagement within public administration (or the justice system), it is unlikely that there would be a unique exception for the implementation of a law with binding effects for corporations. In fact, it may happen that some mining companies could offer--or law enforcement officers request--bribes in exchange for not imposing sanctions against those companies that failed to implement CSR activities. This implies that the implementation of CSR activities in the DRC would still depend on the good faith of companies whether or not the CSR law established drastic sanctions for lack of compliance with its provisions.

Nonetheless, there are also cases where, for example, mining companies in the DRC provided local administrative authorities with small funds to repair schools or other facilities of community interest, and those authorities diverted the funds by using them for their personal interests. I spoke with a former representative of a mining company in Katanga who told me that his former company was requested several times by local authorities to financially contribute to the repair of a small bridge that linked two villages in the vicinity. Although the company provided the funds, that bridge was never repaired and those local authorities were still asking for more money to fix the same bridge without providing any reports about their use of the previous funding. If companies assume that their CSR funds may be mismanaged and utilized for other purposes, it may discourage them from contributing to the social development of local communities.

Regardless of the circumstances, mining companies have a moral obligation[356] to execute their CSR activities beyond the company's financial interests and legal requirements.[357] So, what can the mining companies in the DRC and their clients do to effectively combat child mining labor?

Corporate Actions towards Ending Child Mining Labor

As noted in Chapter Two, the root causes of child mining labor in the DRC consist of a combination of several factors. These factors include poverty, adult unemployment, lack of educational opportunities, globalization with high demand for minerals and cheap labor, and other variables. Of course, to eradicate child mining labor it is imperative to first resolve the causes of these problems. Doing so would naturally require the involvement of all actors, including the government, civil society, and the business sector. In regards to industry's involvement, numerous mining companies and those purchasing from them have currently adopted policies listing their commitments to ethical conduct within their business activities including not using child labor (and/or conflict) minerals in their supply chains.[358] However, there is a difference between pledging the good intention of refraining from using child labor products and translating those intentions into meaningful actions that combat the practice.[359] Even if these intentions are sincere and implemented, they may not be enough to end child mining labor in the DRC. In the context of the DRC, the corporations' monitoring of their mineral supply chains cannot by itself resolve the entire problem of child mining labor. In addition to taking actions to clean their supply chains of child-mined minerals, companies should also implement other incentive programs. These programs may include:

1) Educational incentives to increase children's access to schools in the mining areas. Corporations can support the efforts of local authorities to improve educational systems through building new schools for their employees' children, repairing existing schools, and financing the training of school teachers. Corporations can also provide scholarships and school kits, and implement food-distribution programs at schools in remote mining areas. Researchers have noted that policies that improve the educational system can reduce child labor by increasing its opportunity cost.[360] This is noteworthy because families accept to send their children into the labor force "based partially on the perceived costs and benefits of attending school."[361] Children and their families are therefore less likely to opt for

child labor if education is freely accessible and is a more attractive option.[362]

2) Creation of more job opportunities for adults. Employment creation by corporations can be an important initiative for the development of the local community to the extent that it may not only decrease the high unemployment rate (estimated at 73% of active population in the DRC), but also ensure income generation for both the company and local populations.[363] Mining companies can also develop programs on labor capacity building (including skills training and training partnerships) in order to enable local populations to benefit from the employment opportunities.[364]

3) Financial incentives to reduce poverty. Corporations can assist local authorities in providing financial incentives to poor families in the mining areas, such as credit access and insurance programs. Some economists have observed that, "the relationship between financial market development and child labor is particularly large and robust in poor countries with less developed markets and greater levels of child labor."[365] Others have emphasized that if credit markets allowed households to borrow against future earnings, child labor could be much reduced.[366] As noted in Chapter Two, about 71% of households in the DRC endure credit constraints.[367] Without access to credit, many families are forced to rely on child labor during financial difficulties.[368] Therefore, mining companies can assist the DRC authorities to implement programs that provide credit access to families in poverty so that they could send their children to school instead of working in the artisanal mines.[369]

4) Investment in health care. Mining companies can get more involved in providing health care for their employees and local communities.[370] They could build modern and well-equipped hospitals in the vicinity of their mines; train medical personnel to efficiently deliver services; and establish environmental health and safety programs for their employees.[371] In addition to the humanitarian aspects, it would be financially profitable for mining companies to have a productive and healthy workforce to sustain long-term business growth.[372]

This list of CSR initiatives is not exhaustive. Mining companies could implement a myriad of CSR programs based on their assessment of the priorities and fundamental needs of the communities in which their operations are based. Nevertheless, despite companies' responsibilities in contributing to local development, the burden of eradicating child labor and improving societal quality of life weighs principally on the host government. The contributions of companies can only be subsidiary to governmental policies and laws. In regards to the DRC, the central government should enforce its constitutional provisions on free access to education for all children; provide decent jobs for its citizens; build infrastructures (educational, medical and others) with taxes collected from corporations and other entities; and prosecute those individuals and companies who benefit from child labor.

CONCLUSION

In this book, I endeavor to provide a narrative that exposes the problem of child labor in the mining sector in the DRC. My research suggests that a combination of factors drives children to work in the artisanal mines in the DRC. These variables include poverty, adult unemployment, lack of educational opportunities, sociocultural conditions, lack of law enforcement, and globalization with its high demand for mined minerals and cheap labor. In artisanal mines, children work under dangerous conditions with bare hands and feet, and without protective gear. These dangerous working conditions expose children to the risk of injuries, illnesses, developmental problems, and fatal accidents.

Child miners in the DRC contribute significantly in the production of a variety of raw minerals such as cobalt, coltan, and tin among others. All of these minerals are fundamental elements used in the fabrication of modern electronics. Before these products reach consumers at the end of the chain, the supply chain of child-mined minerals commonly involves intermediaries, mining companies, smelters/refineries, and manufacturers. Employers and buyers have a financial incentive to use child miners or source minerals from them. Based on my calculations, an owner of a mine trading house who buys, exports and resells child-mined cobalt ores on the global market, can make an annual net profit of $4,000,000. This means that child mining labor is a highly profitable business for those who source from children; their expenses are very low and their profits are extremely high. Unfortunately, the benefits are less clear for the child miners, as they earn meager revenues ranging from $0.75 to $3.00 per day while facing numerous risks and missed opportunities for a better life.

In writing this book, a more implicit objective was to prompt greater efforts to prevent child labor in the DRC's mines, to protect vulnerable child victims, and to prosecute those benefiting from child labor exploitation. This being said, the question I pose to readers is: What can you personally do to combat child mining labor? I suggest to you the following actions:

1) Raise awareness: Share the content of this book with your neighbors or colleagues to educate them about child mining labor in the DRC. Inform them that this issue also touches their lives because the electronic devices that they use daily are likely produced with materials tainted with child labor from the DRC.

2) Financial support: Create or support efforts of international NGOs, and domestic NGOs in the DRC, to address the root causes of this scourge. A list of NGOs working on the protection of children is attached in the Appendix F. No matter how small your financial assistance may seem, it can have a huge impact on hundreds of thousands of children in the DRC.

3) Pressure governments: For those of you living in the DRC, put pressure on provincial and national governmental authorities to enforce free access to education for all children and to build more schools so that children can spend more time in schools than in mines.

4) Contact corporations: For those of you living outside of the DRC (Western countries, Asia or elsewhere) write letters to your electronic or automobile manufacturers requesting them to trace their supply chains of raw ores originating from the DRC and avoid using minerals emanating from child labor. In addition to tracing their supply chains, consumers can also encourage manufacturers and suppliers located in the DRC to implement CSR programs to improve the quality of life of local communities in the remote mining regions where their materials come from. Accordingly, manufacturers and suppliers may support the efforts of the DRC authorities to: improve educational systems, make accessible potable water and electricity, provide credit access to poor families, and build hospitals and asphalt roads.

5) Use judicial authority: For those of you serving as prosecutors in the DRC, do not wait to receive a formal complaint or denunciation before prosecuting child mining labor cases. Use the power invested in you by the Code of Judicial Organization and Competence to initiate criminal investigations on your own initiative and bring charges against those who profit from child labor in the mining sectors. For those working in law enforcement outside of the DRC (USA, EU, Canada and elsewhere), impose sanctions based on your domestic laws against corporations in your countries who negligently fail to comply with their legal obligations to disclose their use of tainted minerals coming from the DRC.

6) Use social media: Human rights activists should take advantage of the influence of social media to raise awareness about and lobby against child labor and other forms of child exploitation.

If you execute some or all of these actions and encourage your peers to do so, the fight against child mining labor will be won.

APPENDICES

APPENDIX A

Table 3.3: Health and Nutrition-related MDG Indicators, DRC

	Urban DRC	Rural DRC	DRC	Sub-Saharan Africa
MGD1: Poverty and Hunger				
Prevalence Child Malnutrition (underweight) (% under age 5 years)	22	36	31	30
Prevalence Child Malnutrition (stunting) (% under age 5 years)	29	43	38	41
Prevalence Child Malnutrition (wasting) (% under age 5 years)	12	18	16	10
MDG 4: Child Mortality				
Under-5 Mortality rate (per 1,000 live births)	158	243	220	174
Infant mortality rate (per 1,000 live births)	95	144	128	103
Measles Immunization (% of children ages 12-23 months)	65	40	48	58
MDG 5: Maternal Mortality	---	---	---	
Maternal Mortality Ratio (per 100,000 live births)	---	---	1,289	917
Births Attended by Skilled Health Staff (%)	32	20	24	39
MDG 6: HIV/AIDS, Malaria, and Other Diseases Prevalence of HIV (% Adults aged 15 to 49 prevalence)	---	---	1.1	---
Children aged 0 to 14 Living with HIV			66,000	
Adults aged 15 and older Living with HIV			380,000	
Proportion Sleeping Under Insecticide-Treated Bednets (% children under age 5)	---	---	0.7	2
Proportion of Children with Fever Treated with Anti-Malarials (% children under age 5 with fever)	63	47	52	42
Incidence of Tuberculosis (per 100,000 per year)			384	358
Tuberculosis Cases Detected under DOTS (%)			52	
MDG 7: Environment				
Access to an Improved Water Source (% of population)	84	29	46	58
Access to Improved Sanitation (% of population)	61	39	46	54

Source for the HIV/AIDS data: The United Nations Program on HIV/AIDS (UNAIDS).
Source for all other data: World Bank.

APPENDIX B

Table 4.1: List of the World's Cobalt Consumers & Processors

Rank	Company Name	Country of Origin
1	A.M.P.I. SRL	Italy
2	ATI Allvac	USA
3	Boehler Edelstahl Gmbh	Austria
4	Cannon-Muskegon Corporation	USA
5	Ceratizit SA	Luxembourg
6	Chempro	Europe
7	CRI-Criterion Inc	USA
8	Cytec Industries France	France
9	Daido Kogyo Co Ltd	Japan
10	Deloro Stellite	Italy
11	Designed Alloy Products	USA
12	DIC Corporation	Japan
13	EAC Corp	USA
14	Eurotungstene	France
15	Firth Rixson	United Kingdom
16	Global Tungsten & Powders Co	USA
17	Greatpower Material Technology (Shanghai) Co Ltd	China
18	Hall Chemical	USA
19	Haynes International	USA
20	IBC Advanced Technologies	USA
21	Incasa	South America
22	Johnson Matthey	United Kingdom
23	Kennametal Inc	USA
24	Kogsei	Asia
25	Latrobe Specialty Steel	USA
26	Less Common Metals	United Kingdom
27	LS-Nikko Copper Inc	South Korea
28	MCP-Group	Australia
29	MCM Quimica Industrial Ltd	Brazil
30	Metax Corp	Asia
31	Millenium Alloys	USA
32	Nanjing Hanrui Cobalt Co	China
33	OM Group	USA
34	Panasonic Corporation	Japan
35	Precision Cast Parts	USA
36	Rockwood Pigments	Europe
37	Rolls Royce	United Kingdom
38	Ross & Catherall	United Kingdom
39	Samsung	South Korea

40	Sandvik Tooling	Sweden
41	Seco Tools AB	Europe
42	Shanghai Hengxing Nickel & Cobalt Material Sales	China
43	Shanghai Jitian Investment Group Co	China
44	Shenzhen Gem High-Tech Co	China

Source: London Metal Exchange.

Table 4.2: List of the World's Cobalt Traders and Distributors

Rank	Company Name	Country of Origin
1	AB Ferrolegeringar	Sweden
2	Adee International	South Africa
3	All Metals & Materials, Inc.	USA
4	Ambassador Lushbury Metals	UK
5	Ameropa	Switzerland
6	AS Nordmet	Europe
7	Atlantic Metals & Alloys	USA
8	BenMet NY	USA
9	Darton Commodities	UK
10	Earth Metals	North America
11	Eurochain	Europe
12	Gerli Metalli Spa	Italy
13	Glencore International	UK-Switzerland
14	Great Atlantic Enterprise Inc	Taiwan
15	Hudson Metals Corp	USA
16	Intermetal	Europe
17	Jinchuan (Europe) Ltd	UK
18	Jinchuan (USA) Inc	USA
19	JLI Metals & Commodities Services Sàrl	Switzerland
20	Kohsei Co	Vietnam
21	LC Future International Corporation	Europe/South Africa
22	LN Metals	UK
23	Manatrade	Switzerland
24	Marubeni Corp	Japan
25	Mitsubishi Corporation	Japan
26	Mitsui & Co	Japan
27	MK Import Export	USA
28	MRI Trading AG	Switzerland
29	Ohgitani (Shanghai) Trading Co	China
30	Phoenixx International	USA
31	SFP Metals	UK
32	Shanghai Greatpower Industry Co Ltd	China

33	Specialty Chemical Group	USA
34	Standard Bank	South Africa
35	Stratton Metal Resources	UK
36	Sumitomo Corporation	Japan
37	Todini and Co	Italy
38	Transamine	Switzerland
39	Traxys Belgium	Belgium
40	Traxys North America	USA
41	Trend Capital Limited (Trencome)	Asia
42	Tricor Group	USA
43	William Rowland Ltd	UK
44	Wogen	UK
45	Yano Metals	Japan
46	Zenith Metals	India

Source: London Metal Exchange

Table 4.3: List of Smelters of Tantalum (also known as Coltan)

Rank	Smelter Name	Country of Origin
1	Mineracao Toboca	China
2	Conghua Tantalum and Niobium	China
3	Jiujiang Tangbre Co., Ltd	China
4	Jiangmen Fuxiang Electro-materials Limited (F&X)	China
5	Jiujiang Jinxin Nonferrous Metals Co., Ltd	China
6	Ningxia Orient Tantalum Industry Co., Ltd	China
7	Zhaoqing Duoluoshan Non-ferrous Metals	China
8	Fogang Jiata Metals	China
9	Junde Technology	China
10	King-Tan Tantalum Industry Ltd	China
11	Taike Technology (Suzhou)	China
12	Yichun Jin Yang Rare Metals Co., Ltd	China
13	Zhuzhou Cemented Carbide	China
14	H.C .Starck GmbH	Germany
15	Molycorp Silmet	Estonia
16	Metallurgical Products	India
17	Mitsui Mining and Smelting Co., Ltd	Japan
18	Global Advanced Metals Japan K.K.	Japan
19	H.C. Starck Ltd.	Japan
20	Taki Chemical Co., Ltd.	Japan
21	Solikamsk Magnesium Works	Russia
22	Tantalite Resources	South Africa
23	H.C. Starck GmbH	Thailand
24	Global Advanced Metals	United States

Source: Organization for Economic Co-operation and Development (OECD).

Table 4.4: List of Smelters of Tin

Rank	Smelter Name	Country of Origin
1	Metallo Chimique	Belgium
2	EM Vinto	Bolivia
3	OMSA	Bolivia
4	Complejo Metalurgico Vinto S.A.	Bolivia
5	Senju Metal Industry Co., Ltd.	Bolivia
6	SGS	Bolivia
7	Taboca/Paranapanema	Brazil
8	Mineracao Toboca	Brazil
9	Vale Inco, Ltd	Canada
10	Chile	Chile
11	Yunnan Chengfeng Non-Ferrous Metals Co, Ltd	China
12	Jiangxi Ganzhou Batia Non-Ferrous Metals Power Co, Ltd	China
13	China Tin Group Co.,Ltd	China
14	Mengzi Bofa Mining & Smelting Co.,Ltd	China
15	Gejiu Jinge Mining & Smelting Co.,Ltd	China
16	Kunshan Chengli Tin Co., Ltd	China
17	Yunnan Tin Co., Ltd	China
18	China Tin Group Co.,Ltd Laibin Smelting Factory	China
19	Dongguan Qiandao Tin Co.,Ltd	China
20	Guixi Sanyuan Smelting Chemistry CO.,Ltd	China
21	Shaoxing Tianlong Tin Materials Co.,Ltd	China
22	Yuhuada Tin Co.,Ltd	China
23	Hongqiao Metals (Kunshan) Co.,Ltd	China
24	Shenzhen Jinpin Tin Co.,Ltd	China
25	Chongqing Huahao Smelting Co.,Ltd	China
26	Nankang Huashan Non-ferrous Metals Smelting Factory	China
27	Foshan Nanhai Songgang Hongyang Tin Industry Co., Ltd.	China
28	Shenzhen Anchen Tin Co.,Ltd	China
29	Dongguan Humen Shunmao Tin Co.,Ltd	China
30	Shenzhen Qianzhu New Energy Metals Co.,Ltd	China
31	Zhongshi Metal Co.,Ltd	China
32	Nankan Nanshan	China
33	Primeyoung Metal Ind.(Zhuhai) Co.Ltd	China
34	Primeyoung Metal Ind.(Zhuhai) Co.Ltd	China
35	CNMC(Guangxi) PGMA Co.Ltd	China
36	Hezhou Jinwei Tin Co.,Ltd	China
37	Zhongshan Jinye Smelting Co.,Ltd	China
38	Shanghai Sanlian Powder Smelting Co.,Ltd	China
39	Guangxi Fuchuan Smelting Factory	China
40	Guilin Lingui Huipu Non-ferrous Metals Co.,Ltd	China
41	Shangrao Xuri Smelting Factory	China
42	Kovohute Pribram Nastupnicka, A.S.	CzechRepublic
43	PBT	France
44	CV Duta Putra Bangka	Indonesia
45	CV Justindo	Indonesia
46	CV Makmur Jaya	Indonesia
47	CV Nurjanah	Indonesia
48	CV Prima Timah Utama	Indonesia

49	CV Serumpun Sebalai	Indonesia
50	CV United Smelting	Indonesia
51	PT Alam Lestari Kencana	Indonesia
52	PT Artha Cipta Langgeng	Indonesia
53	PT Babel Inti Perkasa	Indonesia
54	PT Babel Surya Alam Lestari	Indonesia
55	PT Bangka Global Mandiri Internasional	Indonesia
56	PT Bangka Kudai Tin	Indonesia
57	PT Bangka Putra Karya	Indonesia
58	PT Bangka Timah Utama Sejahtera	Indonesia
59	PT Belitung Industri Sejahtera	Indonesia
60	PT Billiton Makmur Lestari	Indonesia
61	PT Bukit Timah	Indonesia
62	PT Donna Kembara Jaya	Indonesia
63	PT DS Jaya Abadi	Indonesia
64	PT Eunindo Usaha Mandiri	Indonesia
65	PT Fang Di Multindo	Indonesia
66	PT HP Metals Indonesia	Indonesia
67	PT Koba Tin	Indonesia
68	PT Mitra Stania Prima	Indonesia
69	PT Refined Bangka Tin	Indonesia
70	PT Sariwiguna Binasentosa	Indonesia
71	PT Stanindo Inti Perkasa	Indonesia
72	PT Sumber Jaya Indah	Indonesia
73	PT Tambang Timah (subsidiary of PT Timah)	Indonesia
74	PT Timah	Indonesia
75	PT Timah Nusantara	Indonesia
76	PT Tinindo Inter Nusa	Indonesia
77	PT Yinchendo Mining Industry	Indonesia
78	Mitsui Mining and Smelting Co., Ltd.	Japan
79	JX Nippon Mining & Metals Co., Ltd.	Japan
80	Mitsubishi Material Corporation	Japan
81	Kosaka Smelting & Refining Co., Ltd.	Japan
82	CHANG SUNG (Hana)	Korea
83	Poongsan Corporation	Korea
84	Hyundai-Steel	Korea
85	POSCO	Korea
86	Malaysia Smelting Corp (MSC). Bhd.	Malaysia
87	Cookson	Malaysia
88	Rahman Hydraulic Tin Sdn Bhd	Malaysia
89	Senju Metal Industry Co., Ltd.	Malaysia
90	Minsur／Minsur S.A.	Peru
91	Amalgamet Inc.	Peru
92	PT. Refined Bangka Tin	Peru
93	Senju Metal Industry Co., Ltd.	Peru
94	Novosibrirsk	Russia
95	CSC Pure Technologies	Russia
96	Pure Technology	Russia
97	Chengfeng Metals Co Pte Ltd	Singapore
98	Electroloy Metal Pte	Singapore
99	Heraeus Materials Singapore Pte Ltd	Singapore

100	Mentok Smelter	Singapore
101	Thailand Smelting & Refining Co Ltd	Thailand
102	Koki Products Co. Ltd.	Thailand
103	PT Bukit Timah	Thailand
104	Senju Metal Industry Co., Ltd.	Thailand
105	Thai Sarco	Thailand
106	Cookson	USA
107	EFD INC.	USA
108	Mansur	USA
109	Taboca	USA
110	Technic Inc.	USA

Source: Organization for Economic Co-operation and Development (OECD).

APPENDIX C

Table 4.6: Application for Coltan (Columbite-Tantalite)

Tantalum Products	Applications
Tantalum carbide	• Cutting tools
Lithium tantalate	• Surface Acoustic Wave (SAW) filters in mobile phones, hi-fi stereos and televisions.
Tantalum oxide	• Lenses for spectacles, digital cameras and mobile phones • X-ray film • Ink jet printers
Tantalum powder	• Tantalum capacitors for electronic circuits in: • Medical appliances such as hearing aids and pacemakers; • Automotive components such as ABS, airbag activation, engine management modules, GPS; • Portable electronics, including laptop computers, cellular/mobile phones, video cameras, and digital still cameras; • Other equipment such as DVD players, flat screen TVs, games consoles, battery chargers, power rectifiers, cellular/mobile phone signal masts, and oil well probes.
Tantalum fabricated sheets and plates	• Chemical process equipment including lining, cladding, tanks, valves, heat exchangers; • Cathodic protection systems for steel structures such as bridges and water tanks; • Corrosion resistant fasteners, screws, nuts and bolts; and • Spinnerettes in synthetic textile manufacture
Tantalum fabricated sheets, plates, rods, wires	• Prosthetic devices for humans - hip joints, skull plates, mesh to repair bone removed after damage by cancer, suture clips, and stents for blood vessels.
Tantalum fabricated sheets, plates, rods, wires	• High temperature furnace parts.
Tantalum ingot	• Sputtering targets.
Tantalum ingot	• High temperature alloys for air and land based turbines (such as jet engine discs, blades and vanes), and rocket nozzles
Tantalum ingot	• Computer hard drive discs.

Source: Tantalum-Niobium International Study Center.

APPENDIX D

Table 4.7: Conflict Minerals Reporting Template

	Conflict Minerals Reporting Template (CMRT)
cfsi An initiative of the EICC and GeSI Select Language Preference Here: 请选择你的语言: 사용할 언어를 선택하시오 : 表示言語をここから選択してください: Sélectionner la langue préférée ici: Selecione Preferência de idioma Aqui: Wählen sie hier die Sprache: Seleccione el lenguaje de preferencia aqui: Selezionare la lingua di preferenza qui:	Revision 3.01 May 30, 2014

The purpose of this document is to collect sourcing information on tin, tantalum, tungsten and gold used in products

Mandatory fields are noted with an asterisk (*). The information collected in this template should be updated annually. Any changes within the annual cycle should be provided to your customers.

Company Information	
Company Name (*):	
Declaration Scope or Class (*):	
Description of Scope:	
Company Unique ID:	
Company Unique ID Authority:	
Address	
Contact Name (*):	
Email – Contact (*):	
Phone – Contact (*):	
Authorizer (*):	
Title - Authorizer:	
Email - Authorizer (*):	
Phone - Authorizer (*):	
Effective Date (*):	

Answer the following questions 1-7 based on the declaration scope indicated above

1) Is the conflict metal intentionally added to your product? (*)	Answer	Comments
Tantalum (*)		
Tin (*)		
Gold (*)		
Tungsten (*)		

2) Is the conflict metal necessary to the production of your company's products and contained in the finished product that your company manufactures or contracts to manufacture? (*)	Answer	Comments
Tantalum (*)		
Tin (*)		
Gold (*)		
Tungsten (*)		

3) Does any of the conflict metal originate from the covered countries? (*)	Answer	Comments
Tantalum (*)		
Tin (*)		
Gold (*)		
Tungsten (*)		

4) Does 100 percent of the conflict metal (necessary to the functionality or production of your products) originate from recycled or scrap sources? (*)	Answer	Comments
Tantalum (*)		
Tin (*)		
Gold (*)		
Tungsten (*)		

5) Have you received conflict metals data/information for each metal from all relevant suppliers of 3TG? (*)	Answer	Comments
Tantalum (*)		
Tin (*)		
Gold (*)		
Tungsten (*)		

6) For each conflict metal, have you identified all of the smelters your company and its suppliers use to supply the products included within the declaration scope indicated above? (*)	Answer	Comments
Tantalum (*)		
Tin (*)		
Gold (*)		
Tungsten (*)		

7) Has all applicable smelter information received by your company been reported in this declaration? (*)	Answer	Comments
Tantalum (*)		
Tin (*)		
Gold (*)		
Tungsten (*)		

Answer the Following Questions at a Company Level		
Question	Answer	Comments
A. Do you have a policy in place that addresses conflict minerals sourcing? (*)		
B. Is your conflict minerals sourcing policy publicly available on your website? (Note – if yes, the user shall specify the URL in the comment field.) (*)		
C. Do you require your direct suppliers to be DRC conflict-free? (*)		
D. Do you require your direct suppliers to source from smelters validated by an independent private sector audit firm? (*)		
E. Have you implemented due diligence measures for conflict-free sourcing? (*)		
F. Do you collect conflict minerals due diligence information from your suppliers which is in conformance with the IPC-1755 Conflict Minerals Data Exchange standard [e.g., the CFSI Conflict Minerals Reporting Template]? (*)		
G. Do you request smelter names from your suppliers? (*)		
H. Do you review due diligence information received from your suppliers against your company's expectations? (*)		
I. Does your review process include corrective action management? (*)		
J. Are you subject to the SEC Conflict Minerals rule? (*)		

Source: Electronic Industry Citizenship Coalition (EICC).

APPENDIX E

National Association of Manufacturers (NAM) vs. Security and Exchange Commission (SEC)

As stated earlier, the SEC regulations for Disclosing Use of Conflict Minerals stipulates that companies should: 1) disclose annually whether their products contain conflict minerals originating from the DRC or its neighboring countries;[373] 2) include in their reports the audits of the supply chain traceability conducted by an independent third party in accordance with the US Comptroller General standards;[374] 3) include information describing all products manufactured or contracted to be manufactured that are not "DRC conflict free;"[375] and 4) submit their report to the SEC by May 31, 2014 for data collected in 2013, and publish their reports on their websites for the public.[376]

In September 2013, approximately nine months prior to the reporting deadline, the NAM approached the U.S. Court of Appeals for the District of Columbia Circuit to challenge the 2012 SEC final rule on Disclosing Use of Conflict Minerals.[377] The NAM told the Court of Appeals that: 1) the SEC had incorrectly interpreted the Dodd-Frank Law requiring the reporting of certain minerals that "did originate" in and around the DRC to cover minerals that "may have originated" from DRC and its neighboring countries;[378] 2) the SEC failed to recognize and use its power to establish a reasonable *de minimis* exception for small amounts of minerals to provide substantial relief from the burdensome requirements of the rule for thousands of manufacturers;[379] and 3) the SEC regulations violated the companies' First Amendment right by requiring them to describe their products as not "DRC conflict free" in the reports they should file with the SEC and post on their websites.[380]

In its April 2014 decision, the Court of Appeals rejected most of the NAM's allegations except the allegation on the violation of the company's First Amendment rights. Three principal inferences may be retained from that opinion of the Court of Appeals, namely:

1) The confirmation of the company's obligation to track and report tainted materials in their products. While confirming the company's duty to publicly disclose their use of conflict minerals, the Court also emphasized that there should not be an established minimum quantity of conflict minerals under which companies should be exonerated from reporting their use of.[381] This means that companies must even report their use of benign amounts of conflict minerals, such as one gram.

2) The reaffirmation of the SEC's right of discretion. The Court upheld that the SEC has a right to exercise its reasonable discretion in the case of ambiguity or silence of the Law.[382] This recognition of the right of discretion may be intended to provide the SEC with ample "margin of maneuver" to regulate unforeseen or unexplained circumstances which may occur in the process of supply chain disclosure.

3) The affirmation that the process of disclosure of use of conflict minerals should not impede the company's First Amendment right. According to the

Court, even if companies are required to disclose their use of conflict minerals, such a disclosure process should not violate the company's freedom of speech.[383] The Court concluded that: "The SEC's final rule violates the First Amendment to the extent the statute and rule require regulated entities to report to the Commission and to state on their website that any of their products have "not been found to be 'DRC conflict free.'"[384] In other words, it is unconstitutional for the SEC to compel companies to criticize their own products as not being "DRC conflict free."

The Court's decision overturning the disclosure requirement should not be understood as discharging the companies from their legal obligation of conducting the traceability of the supply chains of minerals that they use in their products. Rather, the Court decided against the SEC's rule of disclosure, but not Section 1502 of Dodd-Frank Law itself. Therefore, companies must still trace their supply chains and report to the SEC on their use of conflict minerals if the latter revises partially or completely the formulation of the company's public reporting requirement.

APPENDIX F

Anti-child Labor Organizations and Agencies Operating in the DRC

Action Contre l'Impunité pour les Droits de l'Homme (ACIDH)
14 Makomeno, Lubumbashi
Katanga- DR Congo
Phone: + 243 997 025 331/ +243 997 108 022
Website: www.acidhcd.org

ACIDH is a nongovernmental organization dedicated to fighting against impunity for human rights violations. It develops four principal programs, including: the Civil Rights and Policies; the socioeconomic and cultural rights; the rights of women, children and vulnerable people; and the right to peace and sustainable development. ACIDH publishes numerous reports, press releases and other documents on child mining labor and the social responsibilities of mining companies operating in the DRC. It also lodges complaints before the Congolese courts against private mining companies for violation of mine workers' rights.

Alternative Plus
15, Luvungi, Kampemba
Lubumbashi-Katanga
DR Congo
Phone: +243 816 043 745
Alternativesplus.ong@gmail.com

Alternatives Plus is a Katanga-based nonprofit working on the promotion of human rights. Alternatives Plus has been extensively involved in the social reintegration of former child miners and raising awareness of local communities against child labor and sexual abuses in artisanal mines in Katanga. It is partnered with the Provincial Department of Social Affairs on the adoption and implementation of the provincial action plan against the worst forms of child labor in Katanga.

Association Africaine de Défense des Droits de l'Homme (ASADHO)

Katalay Building
12 Avenue de la Paix
Local 1, 1er niveau
Kinshasa / Gombe
DR Congo
Phone: +243 122 16 53
Website: blog.asadho.org

ASADHO is a non-political, non-governmental organization working for human rights in the Democratic Republic of Congo. It was formed in January 1991 in Kinshasa and works to defend human rights through monitoring, reporting and denunciation of killings, torture, rape, maiming, the use of child soldiers and other abuses. The organization has branches throughout the country which compile the information they uncover for inclusion in press releases and reports which ASADHO is then able to bring to the attention of policymakers.

Business for Social Responsibility (BSR)
5 Union Square West, 6th Floor
New York, NY 10003
Phone: +1 212 370 7707
Fax: +1 646 758 8150
Website: www.bsr.org

BSR is a global nonprofit business network dedicated to creating a just and sustainable world. It envisions a world in which everyone can lead a prosperous and dignified life within the boundaries of the Earth's natural resources. BSR has been working with companies to raise their awareness about conflict minerals from the DRC and encourage their involvement in solutions such as iTSCi through multistakeholders convening, working groups, best practice sharing and individual company engagement.

Centre d'Etude et de Formation en Criminologie et droits humains (CEFROCRIM)
Ecole de criminologie
Université de Lubumbashi
Katanga- DR Congo
Phone: + 243 815 977 996

CEFROCRIM is an interdisciplinary center based at the school of criminology at the University of Lubumbashi. It has been involved in research projects on child protection in the mining industry in Katanga. Its principal initiatives on child protection include studying: the problems of child labor in Katanga, conflicts relating to artisanal mining, and capacity-building for paralegal on child protection.

Center for Research on the Environment, Democracy and Human Rights (CREDDHO)
49, Avenue UVIRA, Route de l'ULPGL
Quartier HIMBI II, Commune de Goma, Ville de Goma
Nord-Kivu- DR Congo
Phone: +243811344973 and +243994167279
Website: www.creddho-rdc.org
CREDDHO is a nongovernmental organization working on the promotion and protection of human rights, environment and democracy. It is based in Goma in South Kivu Province in the eastern DRC and implements numerous initiatives, including monitoring and advocacy on modern slavery in the mines.

Comité National de Lutte contre les Pires Formes de Travail des Enfants
(National Committee to Combat the Worst Forms of Child Labor)
Ministère de l'Emploi, du Travail et de la Prévoyance Sociale
Building Kimpoko, Boulevard du 30 Juin
Kinshasa-Gombe
DR Congo
Webiste: www.mintravail.gouv.cd

The National Committee to Combat the Worst Forms of Child Labor is a governmental agency and part of the Ministry of Employment, Labor and Social Welfare. It coordinates activities that include compiling data on the nature and extent of child labor, preventing and rescuing children from engaging in the worst forms of child labor, conducting public awareness campaigns, and building the capacity of government officials and civil society to combat exploitative child labor. The Committee is led by the Ministry of Employment, Labor and Social Welfare. Its members include representatives from the Ministry of Justice, the Ministry of Social Affairs, Humanitarian Action, and National Solidarity, local NGOs, and civil society.

Eastern Congo Initiative (ECI)
3417 Fremont Ave N Suite 400
Seattle WA 98103
Website: www.easterncongo.org

ECI is a nonprofit envisioning an eastern Congo vibrant with abundant opportunities for economic and social development, where a robust civil society can flourish. ECI has been implementing a number of initiatives to support the Congolese organizations, including the grant program. Through its direct grant program, ECI supports local solutions for survivors of rape and sexual violence; and vulnerable children through health, education, and income generation projects. ECI is also involved in programs concerning the returning and reintegrating former child soldiers into their communities.

Enough Project
1333 H Street NW, 10th Floor,
Washington, D.C., 20005.
Phone: +1 310-717-0606
Website: www.enoughproject.org

Enough Project is a nongovernmental organization engaged in ending genocide and crimes against humanity. It focused on areas where some of the world's worst atrocities occur. In connection with the DRC, Enough Project implemented several campaign projects to build the consumer voice for conflict-free electronics, such as cell phones, laptops, and other devices that will not finance war in eastern Congo.

Free the Slaves
P.O Box 34727
Washington, DC 20005
Phone: +1 202 638 1865
Fax: +1 202 638 0599
Website: www.freetheslaves.net

Free the Slaves is a nonprofit organization dedicated to ending slavery around the world. In the DRC, Free the Slaves has been working to combat labor slavery in the mining zones. Its field teams in eastern DRC work to uncover the extent of slavery and to develop ways to end it.

FXB Center for Health and Human Rights
Harvard School of Public Health
651 Huntington Avenue, 7th Floor
Boston, MA 02115 USA
Phone: +1-617-432-0656
Fax: +1-617-432-4310
Website: fxb.harvard.edu

The FXB Center is an interdisciplinary center at Harvard University that works to protect and promote the rights and wellbeing of children, adolescents, youth and their families in extreme circumstances worldwide. In 2012, the Center launched its *Human Trafficking and Forced Labor Program* with the conviction that more effective and sustainable anti-trafficking strategies are critical to address the scourge of human trafficking worldwide. In the DRC, the FXB Center implemented a capacity building program to reinforce the capacity of judges and prosecutors in Katanga to prosecute cases of child labor in the artisanal mines.

Groupe One - Katanga
957 Avenue Lac Kipopo, Lubumbashi
Katanga- DR Congo
Phone: +243 998 494 863
Website: www.groupeone.be

Groupe One is a nongovernmental organization dedicated to conducting research and action on sustainable development and local economic development. Since 2003, it has been active in the DRC where it operates in favor of the emergence of responsible private sector and development actor. Its program on sustainable development in the DRC focuses on the extractive industry. Groupe One also implements projects against child labor in heterogenite artisanal mines in South Katanga.

PACT
1828 L Street, NW, Suite 300
Washington, DC 20036
Phone: +1-202-466-5666
Website: pactworld.org

PACT is a nonprofit enabling systemic solutions that allow those who are poor and marginalized to earn a dignified living, be healthy, and take part in the benefits that nature provides. PACT has been implementing programs on the eradication child labor and conflict minerals in the supply chains of mined minerals in the DRC. It is the lead field implementer for iTSCi (ITRI Tin Supply Chain Initiative) that consists of a comprehensive traceability and due diligence system developed by ITRI (the tin association) and TIC (the tantalum association). PACT also partners with the Governments of the Great Lakes Region to assure tin, tantalum, and tungsten coming from mines in DRC and neighboring countries meet OECD requirements for conflict-free minerals.

Plateforme des Activistes des Droits de l'Homme de Likasi (PADHOLIK)

97, Avenue Kapata, Quartier Kampumpi
Commune de Likasi
Katanga- DR Congo
Phone: +243 99 704 23 86/ + 243 81 211 56 94
padholik@yahoo.fr

PADHOLIK is a nongovernmental organization involved in the promotion and protection of human rights in Likasi in the DRC's province of Katanga. PADHOLIK published several reports and press releases on water pollution by mining companies in Katanga, on child labor in artisanal mines, and conflicts related to artisanal mining.

The Carter Center
One Copenhill
453 Freedom Parkway
Atlanta, GA 30307
Phone: +1 404 420 5100
Website: www.cartercenter.org

The Carter Center is a global organization dedicated to preventing and resolving conflicts, enhancing freedom and democracy, and improving health. Its website contains reports and brochures on child labor in artisanal mines in the DRC. The Carter Center's field office in Katanga also developed a separate website providing specific information on the industrial mining sector in the DRC, including access to natural resources, mining operations, and collection of revenue from the mining operations.

United Nations Children's Fund (UNICEF) - DR Congo
B.P. 7248 Kin 1
Kinshasa- DR Congo
Phone: + 243 815 557 680 /+243 996 050 399
Website: www.unicef.org/drcongo

UNICEF is an agency of the United Nations dedicated to defending, promoting and protecting children's rights. In the DRC, UNICEF has been supporting numerous programs in favor of vulnerable children, including efforts to help child miners to quit the mines and return to school.

Save the Children- DR Congo
10 rue de l'Avenir, Concession CHANIC
Kintambo- Kinshasa
DR Congo
Phone: + 243 880 36 82
Email: scfkinshasa@maf.org
Website: www.savethechildren.maf.org

Save the Children is a nonprofit envisioning a world in which every child attains the right to survival, protection, development and participation. It has been working in the DRC since 1994 and applies a holistic approach to supporting DRC's children: getting children back to school, providing them with healthcare and nutrition support, and protecting them from exploitation and abuse.

World Vision International - DR Congo
B.P. 942
Kinshasa, DR Congo
Phone: +243 810 730 309
Website: www.wvi.org/congo-drc

World Vision is a Christian humanitarian organization dedicated to working with children, families, and their communities worldwide to reach their full potential by tackling the causes of poverty and injustice. World Vision started working in the DRC in 1984, where it has been developing programs on transformational development (in the south and the west regions), and humanitarian and emergency response (in the eastern region). Several thousands of children in the DRC benefit from the World Vision's transformational development programs which include education, health care, water and sanitation, nutrition, food security and Christian Commitments.

REFERENCES

Book, Articles and Reports

Action Contre l'Impunité pour les Droits de l'Homme. *Les Investissements Privés et Publics Chinois dans le Secteur Minier au Katanga: Bonne Gouvernance et Droit de l'Homme. Rapport*, 2010.

African Economic Outlook. *Congo, Democratic Republic* (2012).

Agbu, Osita. Children and Youth in the Labour Process in Africa. Codesria: 2009.

Alber, Erdmute, Martin, Jeannett, and Notermans, Catrien. Child Fostering in West Africa: New Perspectives on Theory and Practices. Leiden-Boston: Brill, 2013.

Allais, Federico, and Hagemann, Frank. "Child Labour and Education: Evidence from SIMPOC Surveys."International Labor Organization, 2008.

BBC News. "Glencore Linked to Acid Waterfall in DR Congo." *BBC News* (April 16, 2012). http://www.bbc.com/news/business-17726865

Bale, Kevin, and Soodalter, Ron. *The Slave Next Door: Human Trafficking and Slavery in America Today*. California: University of California Press, 2009.

Bass, Loretta. *Child Labor in Sub-Saharan Africa*. Colorado: Lynne Rienner Publishers, 2004.

Basu, Kaushik, and Hoang, Pham V. "Economics of Child Labor." *American Economic Review* 88, no.3 (1998): 412–427.

Beamon, Benita. "Supply Chain Design and Analysis: Models and Methods." *International Journal of Production Economics* 55, no.3 (1998): 281–294.

Bharti, Sarita, and Agarwal, Shalini. "Physical and Psychological Hazards Faced by Child Labour—A Review Article." *IOSR Journal of Humanities and Social Science* 13, no 6 (2013): 29–33.

Bird, Chris. "The hard road to healthcare for eastern Congo's poor." *The Guardian.* (10 April 2012). http://www.theguardian.com/global-development/poverty-matters/2012/apr/10/hard-road-healthcare-congo-poor

Bray, Nicholas. "Minerals Not to Die For." http://www.oecdobserver.org/news/fullstory.php/aid/3801/Minerals_not_to_die_for.html

Brown, Gordon. "Child Labour and Educational Disadvantage—Breaking the Link, Building Opportunity," (2012): 35.

Carolease, Beverly G. *Invisible Hands: Child Labor and the State in Colonial Zimbabwe*. New Hampshire: Social History of Africa, 2006.

Casey-Maslen, Stuart. *The War Report: Armed Conflict in 2013.* (Oxford University Press, 2014).

Central Intelligence Agency. "The World Factbook." https://www.cia.gov/library/publications/the-world-factbook/fields/2127.html

Child Labor Public Education Project. "What is Child Labour?"
    https://www.continuetolearn.uiowa.edu/laborctr/child_labor/about/what_is_
    child_labor.html

Cobalt Development Institute. "Cobalt Facts." www.thecdi.com/cobaltfacts.php

ECOMIN mining model. "Traceability of minerals."
    http://www.ecomin.co/traceable_minerals.html

Dahlsrud, Alexander. "How Corporate Social Responsibility is Defined: An
    Analysis of 37 Definitions." *Wiley InterScience* (2006): 1–13.

Dowling, Samantha, Moreton, Karen, and Wright, Leila. "Trafficking for the
    Purposes of Labour Exploitation: A literature Review." *Home Office Online
    Report* (2007).
    http://webarchive.nationalarchives.gov.uk/20110218135832/rds.homeoffice
    .gov.uk/rds/pdfs07/rdsolr1007.pdf

Ebbe, Obi N. I., and Das, Dilip K. *Global Trafficking in Women and Children*. New
    York: CRC Press, 2008.

Ebigbo, Peter et al. *Child Labour in Africa*. Nigeria: African Network for the
    Prevention and Protection against Child Abuse and Neglect, 1986.

Edmonds, Eric, and Pavcnik, Nina. "Child Labor in the Global Economy." *Journal
    of Economic Perspectives* 19, no 1 (2005): 199–220.

Electronic Industry Citizenship Coalition. "History-EICC."
    http://www.eiccoalition.org/about/history/

Elenge, Myriam, Leveque, Alain, and de Brouwer, Christophe. "Occupational
    Accidents in Artisanal Mining in Katanga, DRC." *International Journal of
    Occupational Medicine and Environmental Health* 26, no.2 (2013): 265–
    274.

Elenge, Myriam, and de Brouwer, Christopher. "Problems of Pathologies related to
    Toxicological Risks in Small Scale Mining. Case of Katanga Province
    (D.R.C.): A Review of the Literature." *Journal International de Santé de
    Travail*, no.1 (2010):28–39.

Esguerra, Emmanuel. *An Analysis of the Causes and Consequences of Child Labor
    in the Philippines*. International Labor Organization (2003).

Environmental Health Perspectives. "Quicksilver and Gold: Mercury Pollution from
    Artisanal and Small-Scale Gold Mining." http://ehp.niehs.nih.gov/120-
    a424/

European Union. "Corporate Social Responsibility."
    http://ec.europa.eu/enterprise/policies/sustainable-business/corporate-
    social-responsibility/index_en.htm

Facing Finance. "Glencore: Environmental Damage, Human Rights Violations, Tax
    Dodging at Katanga." *Facing Finance*.
    http://www.facing-finance.org/en/database/cases/katanga-mining/

Fallon, Nicole. "What is Corporate Social Responsibility?" *Business News Daily*,
    (December 22, 2014). http://www.businessnewsdaily.com/4679-corporate-
    social-responsibility.html

Farooq, Mariam, Farooq, Omer, and Jasimuddin, Sajjad. "Employees Response to
    Corporate Social Responsibility: Exploring the Role of Employees'

Collectivist Orientation." *European Management Journal* 32 (2014):916–927.

Geoview. "Musonoi." http://cd.geoview.info/musonoi,922414

Gordon, Jamie. "The Economic Implications of Child Labor: A Comprehensive Approach to Labor Policy." Duke University (2008).

Graitcer, Philip, and Lerer, Leonard. *Child Labor and Health: Quantifying the Global Health Impacts of Child Labor*. World Bank (1998) 12.

Gunn, Susan. "Combating Child Labour in Congo." BMS World Mission. http://www.bmsworldmission.org/news-blogs/blogs/combating-child-labour-congo

Hamat, Dena, and Tribbett, John. "A Comparative Analysis of Human Trafficking Legislation and Case Law: Suggestions for Best Practices in Creating Laws Against Human Trafficking." *UNODC Publication*, R76 Project (2009).

Hawkins, Virgil. "Stealth Conflicts: Africa's World War in the DRC and International Consciousness." *The Journal of Humanitarian Assistance*. https://sites.tufts.edu/jha/archives/71.

Hilhorst, Dorothea. *Disaster, Conflict and Society in Crisis: Everyday Politics of Crisis Response*. (Abingdon: Routledge Humanitarian Studies, 2013).

History World. "The Democratic Republic of Congo: Congo Free State: 1885–1908." http://www.historyworld.net/wrldhis/PlainTextHistories.asp?historyid=ad34

Human Rights Watch. "Ghana: Mine Accident Highlights Risk to Children." http://www.hrw.org/news/2013/06/13/ghana-mine-accident-highlights-risk-children

International Business Times. "DR Congo's Witchcraft Epidemic: 50,000 Children Accused of Sorcery."www.ibtimes.co.uk/branded-witch-bbc-democratic-republic-congo-kindoki-469216

International Labor Organization and International Programme on the Elimination of Child Labor. *Marking Progress against Child Labour: Global Estimates and Trends 2000–2012*. Geneva: International Labor Office, 2013.

ILO/IPEC-SIMPOC. "Explaining the Demand and Supply Chain of Child Labour: A Review of Underlying Theories" (2007).

International Labour Organization. "What is Child Labour?" http://www.ilo.org/ipec/facts/lang--en/index.htm

———. "The Effective Abolition of Child Labour." (2000).

Investment Mines. http://www.infomine.com/investment/metal-prices/cobalt/

Janssson, Johanna. "CSR Practice in the DRC's Mining Sector by Chinese Firms." *Policy Brief* 9, (2010).

Jeune Afrique. "La RDC reporte l'embargo sur les exportations de minerais." *Jeune Afrique*. http://economie.jeuneafrique.com/regions/afrique-subsaharienne/18438-la-rdc-reporte-lembargo-sur-les-exportations-de-minerais.html

John, Cindi. "Exorcisms are Part of our Culture." *BBC News*, June 3, 2005.

Kara, Siddharth. *Bonded Labor: Tracking the System of Slavery in South Asia.* New York: Columbia University Press, 2012.

———. "Designing More Effective Laws Against Human Trafficking." *Northwestern Journal of International Human Rights* 9, no.2 (2011): 123–147.

———. *Sex Trafficking: Inside the Business of Modern Slavery.* New York: Columbia University Press, 2009.

Kayongo-Male, Diane, and Walji, Parveen. *Children at Work in Kenya.* Nairobi: Oxford University Press, 1984.

Kielland, Anne, and Tovo, Maurizia. *Children at Work: Child Labor Practices in Africa.* Colorado: Lynne Rienner Publishers, 2006.

Keo, Chenda. *Human Trafficking in Cambodia.* New York: Routledge, 2014.

Krueger, Alan. "Observations on International Labor Standards and Trade," NBER Working Paper 5632 (1996).

Kyamwami, Prince. "Travail des Enfants dans le Site Minier d'Exploitation Artisanale de Bisie en Territoire de Walikale: Une Crise Oubliée en République Démocratique du Congo." Bureau d'Etudes, d'Observation et de Coordination pour le Développement du Territoire de Walikale (2003).

Linedecker, Clifford L. *Children in Chains.* New York: Everest House, 1981.

Liwanga, Roger-Claude. "Adopting an Anti-human Trafficking Law in DR Congo: A Significant Step in the Process of Combating Trafficking." *Slavery Today—A Multidisciplinary Journal of Human Trafficking Solutions* 1, no1 (2014): 13–45.

———. "Child Miners Face Death for Tech." *CNN Freedom Project*, June 26, 2013.

———."Economics of Child Mining Labor: Estimation of Corporations Profits." *Slavery Today—A Multidisciplinary Journal of Human Trafficking Solutions* 1, no.2 (2014): 119–133.

Local. "Exorcism Punishes Kids for Family's Woes," *The Local.* http://www.thelocal.se/20130514/47886

Lovells, Hogan, Hilton, Paul, and Tsu, Lillian."Private Companies Now Subject to Sanctions for Purchasing Conflict Minerals." *Lexology.* http://www.lexology.com/library/detail.aspx?g=b3344acf-b9b7-481f-a0c9-775e31b48215

Mgbako, A. Chi and Glenn, Katherine. "Witchcraft Accusation and Human Rights: Case Studies from Malawi," *Geo. Wash. Int'l L. Rev.* 43 (2011): 389–417.

Maybee, Bryan, Mungaven, Melissa, Polukhina, Kseniya, and Bagent, Brandi. "Psychological Impact." *Global Child Labor.* https://sites.google.com/site/globalchildlabor/psychological-impact

Mayundo, Franck M. "Exploitation Minière au Sud Kivu: De la Responsabilité des Entreprises et l'Etat." Licence Diss., Université CEPROMAD Bukavu, 2006.

Meger, Sara. "Rape of the Congo: Understanding Sexual Violence in the Conflict in the Democratic Republic of Congo." *Journal of Contemporary African Studies* 28 (2010), 119–135.

Melcher, Frank, et al. "Fingerprinting of conflict minerals: columbite-tantalite ("coltan") ores." *Society of Geology Applied to Mineral Deposits*, News 23 (2008).

Mineral Education Coalition. "Cobalt." http://www.mineralseducationcoalition.org/minerals/cobalt

Ministère du Travail, de l'Emploi, de la Formation Professionnelle et du Dialogue Social. "Protection des Jeunes Travailleurs." http://www.travailler-mieux.gouv.fr/Protection-de-la-sante-des-jeunes.html

Mollel, Andrew. "International Adjudication and Resolution of Armed Conflicts in the Africa's Great Lakes: A Focus on the DRC Conflict." *Journal of Law and Conflict Resolution* 10 (2009): 10-29.

Mukendi, Emery W., Kempen, Jonathan V., and Kalema, Fulgence B. "L'Interdiction d'Exportation de Concentrés de Cuivre et Cobalt en RDC Sous Analyse." http://www.lexology.com/library/detail.aspx?g=60d620e7-5275-44ce-98e8-aef48d99e8ee

Muayila, Henry, and Tollens, Eric. "Assessing the Impact of Credit Constraints on Farm Household Economic Welfare in the Hinterland of Kinshasa, Democratic Republic of Congo." *African Journal of Food, Agriculture, Nutrition and Development* 12, no 3 (2012). Banque Mondiale. *Le Système Educatif de la République Démocratique du Congo: Priorités et Alternatives* (2005).

Mzembe, Andrew, and Downs, Yvonne. "Managerial and Stakeholder Perceptions of an Africa-based Multinational Mining Company's Corporate Social Responsibility." *The Extractive Industries and Society* 1 (2014): 225–236.

National Association of Manufacturers vs. Security and Exchange Commission (District of Columbia Circuit) No. 13-5252 (2014).

New Mexico Bureau Geology and Mineral Resources. "What Decision Makers Should Know About Soils in New Mexico." https://geoinfo.nmt.edu/geoscience/hazards/collabsible.html

Nguya, Kilondo Didier. "Ménages Gécamines, Précarité et Economie Populaire." DEA diss., Université Catholique de Louvain, 2004.

Nordband, Sara, and Bolme, Petter. *Powering the Mobile World: Cobalt Production for Batteries in the Democratic Republic of Congo and Zambia*. Swedwatch (2007), 30–32.

Oeko-Institut e.V. "Recycling critical raw materials from waste electronic equipment." http://www.oeko.de/oekodoc/1294/2011-419-en.pdf

Organization for Economic Cooperation and Development. "Measuring Productivity: Measurement of Aggregate and Industry-Level Productivity Growth." *OECD Publishing* (2001).

———. "The OECD Due Diligence Guidance for Responsible Supply Chains of Minerals from Conflict-Affected and High-Risk Areas: Second Edition." *OECD Publishing* (2013).

PACT. *Promines Study: Artisanal Mining in the Democratic Republic of Congo* (2010).

Plateforme des Organisations de la Société Civile Intervenant dans le Secteur Minier au Katanga."Propositions d'Amendement du Code Minier." June 2012.

Phiri, Isaac. "Saving Witches in Kolwezi: Accused of Witchcraft by Parents and Churches, Children in the Democratic Republic of Congo are Being Rescued by Christian Activists." *Christianity Today* 53, no. 9 (2009): 62-65.

Poole, Hannah H., Hayes, Karen, and Kacapor, Azra. *Breaking the Chain: Ending the Supply of Child-mined Minerals.* PACT (2013).

Quinlivan, Steve. "UN Report Indicates Continued Smuggling of Conflict Minerals in DRC Region." *Dodd-Frank.* http://dodd-frank.com/un-report-indicates-continued-smuggling-of-conflict-minerals-in-drc-region/

Rafferty, Yvonne. "The Impact of Trafficking on Children: Psychological and Social Policy Perspectives." *Child Development Perspectives* 2, no 1 (2008): 13–18.

Ranängen, Helena, and Zobel, Thomas. "Revisiting the 'How' of Corporate Social Responsibility in Extractive Industries and Forestry." *Journal of Cleaner Production* 84 (2014): 299–312.

Raufflet, Emmanuel, Cruz, Luciano, and Bres, Luc. "An Assessment of Corporate Social Responsibility Practices in the Mining and Oil and Gas Industries." *Journal of Cleaner Production* 84(2014): 256–270.

Rodgers, Gerry, and Standing, Guy. *Child Work, Poverty and Underdevelopment.* Geneva: International Labour Organization, 1981.

Srivastava, Ravi. "Bonded Labour in India: Its Incidence and Pattern." *Cornell University ILR School* (2005). http://digitalcommons.ilr.cornell.edu/forcedlabor/18/

Sweeney, John. "Mining Giant Glencore Accused in Child Labour and Acid Dumping Row," *The Guardian.* http://www.theguardian.com/business/2012/apr/14/glencore-child-labour-acid-dumping-row

Tuttle, Carolyn. *Hard at Work in Factories and Mines: The Economics of Child Labor During the British Industrial Revolution.* Colorado: Westview Press, 1999.

UNAIDS. "The Democratic Republic of Congo." http://www.unaids.org/en/regionscountries/countries/democraticrepublicofthecongo/

UNICEF. "In DR Congo, UNICEF supports efforts to help child labourers return to school." http://www2.unicef.org:60090/infobycountry/drcongo_62627.html

UNDP. "Multidimensional Poverty Index."http://hdr.undp.org/en/content/table-6-multidimensional-poverty-index-mpi

UN Gift. "Trafficking for Forced Labour." http://www.ungift.org/knowledgehub/en/about/trafficking-for-forced-labour.html

United States Department of Labor. "Wage and Hour Division." www.dol.gov/whd/regs/compliance/whdfs43.htm

United States Department of State. "Trafficking in Persons Report 2011."
        http://www.state.gov/j/tip/rls/tiprpt/2011/164231.htm

———. "Trafficking in Persons Report 2012."
        http://www.state.gov/j/tip/rls/tiprpt/2012/192366.htm

United States Securities and Exchange Commission. "The Investor's Advocate: How
        the SEC Protects Investors, Maintains Market Integrity, and Facilitates
        Capital Formation."
        http://www.sec.gov/about/whatwedo.shtml#.VJGQvnvg_-M

United States Department of Labor. "Labor Productivity and Costs."
        http://www.bls.gov/lpc/

US Government Accountability Office. "Report to Congressional Committees on
        SEC Conflict Minerals Rule Department of Labor 2016."
        http://www.gao.gov/assets/680/679232.pdf

———. "Report to Congressional Committees on SEC Conflict Minerals Rule
        Department of Labor 2015." http://www.gao.gov/assets/680/672051.pdf

University of Central Arkansas. "What is a Supply Chain?"
        www.sbaer.uca.edu/publications/supply_chain_management/pdf/01.pdf

Van den Anker, Christian, and Van Liempt, Ilse. *Human Rights and Migration:
        Trafficking for Forced Labor*. United Kingdom: Palgrave Macmillan, 2012.

Van Look, F.A. Paul, Heggenhougen, Kristian and Quah, R., Stella. *Sexual and
        Reproductive Health: A Public Health Perspective*. (San Diego : Academic
        Press, 2011).

Woodhead, Martin. "Psychosocial Impacts of Child Work: A Framework for
        Research, Monitoring and Intervention." *International Journal of
        Children's Rights* 12, no.4 (2004): 321–377.

World Bank. "Data." http://data.worldbank.org/indicator/SE.XPD.PRIM.PC.ZS

———. *Democratic Republic of Congo Growth with Governance in the Mining
        Sector*. (2008), 57.

———. *Democratic Republic of Congo: Health, Nutrition and Populaton* (2005).

World Business Council for Sustainable Development. "Corporate Social
        Responsibility: Making Good Business Sense." (2000).

World Vision. "It is a Corporate Responsibility to Address Forced and Child Labour,
        Not Mine. Discuss." (2012).

———. *Child Miners Speak: Key Findings on Children and Artisanal Mining in
        Kambove DRC* (2013).

World Without Genocide. "Democratic Republic of Congo."
        http://worldwithoutgenocide.org/genocides-and-conflicts/congo.

Zeleza, T. Paul. "Introduction: The Causes and Costs of War in Africa From
Liberation Struggles to the 'War on Terror'" *in The Roots of African Conflicts: The
Causes and Costs and The Resolution of African Conflicts: The Management of
Conflict Resolution and Post-Conflict Reconstruction*. (Athens: Ohio University
Press, 2008): 1-35.

Legal Documents

Constitution of the Democratic Republic of Congo of 2006 as amended by the Law of January 20, 2011 [Constitution de la République Démocratique du Congo tel que modifiée par la Loi du 20 janvier 2011].

Convention concerning Forced or Compulsory Labour of 1930.

Decree No 038/2003 of March 26, 2003 on the Mining Regulations in the Democratic Republic of Congo [Decret No 038/2003 du 26 Mars 2003 portant Réglement Minier en République Démocratique du Congo].

Executive Order 13671—Taking Additional Steps to Address the National Emergency With Respect to the Conflict in the Democratic Republic of the Congo. Federal Register, Vol.79, no.132, July 10, 2014.

French Labor Code as modified by the Law No2011-893 of July 28, 2011 [Code du Travail Français tel que modifié par la Loi N°2011-893 du 28 Juillet 2011].

Inter-ministerial Decree No 122/CAB.MINE/MINES/01/2013 and No782/CAB.MIN/FINANCES/2013 on the Regulation of the Export of Retailing Products in the Democratic Republic of Congo [Arrêté Interministeriel No 122/CAB.MINE/MINES/01/2013 and No782/CAB.MIN/FINANCES/2013 portant Réglementation des Exportations des Produits Marchands en République Démocratique du Congo].

Inter-ministerial Decree N° 3154/CAB.MIN/MINES/01/2007 and N° 031/CAB.MIN/FINANCES/2007 of August 9, 2007 on the Fixing of the Rates of Fees, Taxes and Charges to be Levied on the Initiative of the Minister of Mines [Arrêté interministériel N° 3154/CAB.MIN/MINES /01/2007 et N° 031/CAB.MIN/FINANCES/2007 du 09 août 2007 portant Fixation des Taux des Droits, Taxes et Redevances à Percevoir sur l'Initiative du Ministre des Mines].

Law 06/018 amending and completing the Decree of January 30, 1940 relating to the Congolese Penal Code [Loi N° 06/018 du 20 juillet 2006 modifiant et complétant le Décret du 30 janvier 1940 portant Code Pénal Congolais].

Law 015-2002 of October 16, 2002 on the Congolese Code of Labor [Loi N° 015-2002 du 16 octobre 2002 Portant Code du Travail Congolais].

Law No 007/2002 of July 11, 2002 relating to the Congolese Mining Code [Loi N° 007/2002 du 11 juillet 2002 portant Code Minier Congolais].

Law 09/001 of January 10, 2009 on the Protection of the Child in the Democratic Republic of Congo [Loi No 09/001 du 10 Janvier 2009 portant Protection de l'Enfant en République Démocratique du Congo].

Law 015-2002 of October 2002 on the Congolese Labor Code [Loi No 015-2002 du 16 Octobre 2002 portant Code du Travail Congolais].

Ministerial Decree No 3748 MFPTEOP-DTSS of June 6, 2003 relating to Child Labor in Senegal [Arrêté Ministeriel No 3748 MFPTEOP-DTSS du 6 Juin 2003 relatif au Travail des Enfants au Senegal].

Ministerial Order 12/CAB.MIN/TPSI/045/08 of August 8, 2008 on the Working Conditions of Children in the Democratic Republic of Congo [Arrêté

Ministériel N° 12/CAB.MIN/TPSI/045 /08 du 08 août 2008 fixant les Conditions de Travail des Enfants en République Démocratique du Congo].

Office of Foreign Asset Control, "Democratic Republic of Congo Sanctions Program" August 13, 2013.

Ordinance-Law 82-020 of March 31, 1982 on the Code of Organization and Judicial Competence in the Democratic Republic of Congo [Ordonnance-Loi No 82-020 du 31 Mars 1982 portant Code d'Organisation et Compétence Judiciaire en République Démocratique du Congo].

Legislative Ordinance No 067/310 of August 9, 1967 on the Labor Code [Ordonnance-loi No 067/310 du 9 Août 1967 portant Code du Travail].

Protocol to Prevent, Suppress and Punish Trafficking in Persons, Especially Women and Children of November 15, 2000.

Securities and Exchanges Commission, "Rule for Disclosing Use of Conflict Minerals," August 2012, 17 CFR PARTS 240 and 249b, [Release No. 34-67716; File No. S7-40-10], RIN 3235-AK84.

Section 1502 of the Dodd-Frank Wall Street Reform and Consumer Protection Act.

Supplementary Convention on the Abolition of Slavery, the Slave Trade, and Institutions and Practices similar to Slavery of April 30, 1956.

STYLE SHEET

Vocabulary

- *carte de négociant* are valid trader's cards (chapter 4)
- *comptoirs agréés* are authorized mine trading houses (in contrast to *négociants*) (chapter 4)
- *comptoirs* are trading houses (chapter 4)
- *comptoirs d'achat* are mine trading houses (chapter 1)
- Congolese is the name for the people of the Democratic Republic of Congo
- *creuseur* is a mine digger (chapter 1)
- *de minimis* (chapter 4)
- Dodd-Frank Law (chapter 4)
- *kindoki* means a black magic power (chapter 2)
- *laveur* is the term for children who perform the cleaning of minerals and it means "washer" (chapter 3)
- *Mbazi* is the name of copper ores in the Swahili language (chapter 3)
- *mwana-umé* means a "brave child" in Swahili (chapter 2)
- *mwana-umé* means brave man (chapter 3)
- *négociants* are mine traders (chapter 1)
- Palermo Protocol is the 2000 United Nations Protocol to Prevent, Suppress and Punish Trafficking in Persons, Especially Women and Children (chapter 1)
- *Parquet de Grande Instance* is the Office of the Public Prosecutor (chapter 2)
- *Porteur* is one name for children whose tasks include carrying ores (there are three names) (chapter 3)
- *Saliseur* is one name for children whose tasks include carrying ores (there are three names) (chapter 3)
- *Transporteur* is one name for children whose tasks include carrying ores (there are three names) (chapter 3)
- *Tribunal de Paix* is the Tribunal of Peace (chapter 2)
- *wabulé* means "a weak or useless person" in Swahili (chapter 2)
- *zone d'exploitation artisanale* are artisanal mining zones (chapter 4)

Terms related to minerals, ores, and metals:

- cobalt
- coltan (abbreviation for columbite-tantalite)
- copper
- heterogenite
- superalloy
- tin
- uranium
- WD-X-ray fluorescence
- X-ray diffraction
- zinc

Location names:

- Canada
- Dilala
- Europe
- Goma
- Japan
- Kasai Oriental
- Katanga
- Kinshasa
- Kolwezi
- Lubumbashi
- Lwambo
- Mali
- Musompo
- Musonoi
- North Kivu
- Senegal
- Shinkolobwe mine
- Terre Jaune
- Zambia

Companies:

- Gécamines is a state-owned mining company whose full name is *La Générale des Carrières et des Mines*; it is sometimes spelled GÉCAMINES but this paper standardized on the mixed upper- and lower-case spelling.
- Glencore is a Swiss-based mining company

Acronyms:

- ACIDH = *Action Contre l'Impunité pour les Droits de l'Homme* (an NGO in the DRC)
- CSR = corporate social responsibility
- DRC = Democratic Republic of Congo
- EIA = environmental impact assessment
- GDP = gross domestic product
- ILO = International Labour Organization
- MGD = Millennium Development Goals
- NAM = National Association of Manufacturers
- NGO = nongovernmental organization
- OECD = Organization for Economic Co-operation and Development
- OFAC = Office of Foreign Asset Control
- SEC = Securities and Exchange Commission
- STD = sexually transmitted disease

- UNICEF = United Nations Children's Fund (was the United Nations International Children's Emergency Fund before being shortened 1953)
- UNPA = United Nations Participation Act
- WBCSD = World Business Council for Sustainable Development

Measurements:

- Kilograms (converted to pounds and tons)
- Meters (converted to feet)

Languages

- American English
- British English
- French (extensive usage of French in notes and references, not listed in this style sheet)
- Swahili
- Latin

ENDNOTES

PREFACE – Endnotes

[1] International Labor Organization, International Programme on the Elimination of Child Labor, *Marking Progress against Child Labour: Global Estimates and Trends 2000–2012* (Geneva: International Labor Office, 2013), 3 (hereafter cited as "ILO-IPEC, *Marking Progress*").

[2] Ibid.

[3] Roger-Claude Liwanga, "Economics of Child Mining Labor: Estimation of Corporations Profits," *Slavery Today--A Multidisciplinary Journal of Human Trafficking Solutions* 1, no.2 (2014): 120.

[4] Ibid. Also: World Vision, *Child Miners Speak: Key Findings on Children and Artisanal Mining in Kambove DRC* (Kinshasa: World Vision DR Congo, 2013), 10.

[5] Oeko-Institut e.V., "Recycling critical raw materials from waste electronic equipment," February 24, 2012, http://www.oeko.de/oekodoc/1294/2011-419-en.pdf

[6] Liwanga, "Economics," 129.

[7] In the context of the DRC's decentralization process in 2015, the province of Katanga was administratively split into four small provinces while I was finalizing this book. Since June 2015, the province of Katanga is dismantled in four sub-provinces: Tanganyika, Haut-Lomami, Lualaba and Haut-Katanga. See: Article 2 of the DRC Constitution of 2006 (as revised). See also: Tresor Kibangula, "Décentralisation: le Katanga, un géant démembré," *Jeune Afrique.* http://www.jeuneafrique.com/mag/241412/politique/decentralisation-le-katanga-un-geant-demembre/

[8] Liwanga, "Economics," 125.

[9] Ibid.

[10] International Labour Organization, "What is Child Labour," (n.d.) (hereafter cited as "ILO, 'What is Child Labour'"). http://www.ilo.org/ipec/facts/lang--en/index.htm.

CHAPTER 1 - Endnotes

[11] The United Nations Convention on the Rights of the Child of 1989, Article 1. African Charter on the Rights and Welfare of the Child of 1990, Article 2.

[12] Article 1 of the Decree of December 6, 1950 on Juvenile Delinquency [Décret du 6 décembre 1950 sur l' Enfance délinquante].

[13] Article 3 (a) of Ordinance-Law No 67/310 of August 9, 1967 on the Labor Code (as modified in December 31, 1996) [Ordonnance-Loi No. 67/310 du 9 Août 1967 constituent le Code du Travail, dans sa teneur modifiée au 31 décembre 1996] prohibited the employment of children aged under 14; but it authorized the employment of children between 14 and 16 years of age to solely execute healthy and unhazardous work. The Law was silent about the nature of work be performed

by persons aged between 16 and 18. This leads to the conclusion that individuals aged above 16 years could execute any kind of work.

[14] Article 219 of the Law No. 87-010 of August 1st, 1987 on Family Code [Loi No 87-010 du 1er août 1987 portant Code de la Famille].

[15] Id., Article 352. The minimum age to get married is 15 years for women and 18 years for men.

[16] Id., Article 289.

[17] Id., Article 288 and 292.

[18] Law No. 09/001 of January 10, 2009 on the Protection of the Child [Loi n° 09/001 du 10 Janvier 2009 portant Protection de l'Enfant], Article 2 (1).

[19] Id., Article 48.

[20] Id., Article 84

[21] Id., Article 54.

[22] Osita Agbu, *Children and Youth in the Labour Process in Africa* (Codesria, 2009), 12.

[23] Erdmute Alber, Jeannett Martin, and Catrien Notermans, *Child Fostering in West Africa: New Perspectives on Theory and Practices* (Leiden-Boston: Brill, 2013), 33-34.

[24] Hannah Poole Hahn, Karen Hayes, and Azra Kacapor, *Breaking the Chain: Ending the Supply of Child-mined Minerals* (Washington, DC: Pact, 2013), 25.

[25] Liwanga, "Adopting," 17.

2626

[27] International Labour Organization, "What is Child Labour," (n.d.) (hereafter cited as "ILO, 'What is Child Labour'"), http://www.ilo.org/ipec/facts/lang--en/index.htm.

[28] Ibid.

[29] Ibid.

[30] Ibid. Also: Child Labor Public Education Project, "What is Child Labour?" (2011). https://www.continuetolearn.uiowa.edu/laborctr/child_labor/about/what_is_child_labor.html

[31] United State Department of Labor, "Wage and Hour Division," (2010). http://www.dol.gov/whd/regs/compliance/whdfs43.htm

[32] Code du Travail Français tel que modifié par la Loi N°2011-893 du 28 Juillet 2011 [French Labor Code as modified by the Law No2011-893 of July 28, 2011], http://www.legifrance.gouv.fr/affichCodeArticle.do?idArticle=LEGIARTI00000690 3179&cidTexte=LEGITEXT000006072050

[33] Id., Article L4153-1.

[34] Arrêté Ministeriel No 3748 MFPTEOP-DTSS du 6 Juin 2003 relatif au Travail des Enfants au Senegal [Ministerial Decree No 3748 MFPTEOP-DTSS of June 6, 2003 relating to Child Labor in Senegal], http://www.jo.gouv.sn/spip.php?article735

[35] Id., Article 1.

[36] ILO, "The Effective Abolition of Child Labour," (2000), 291, http://www.google.com/url?sa=t&rct=j&q=&esrc=s&source=web&cd=1&ved=0CB4QFjAA&url=http%3A%2F%2Fwww.ilo.org%2Fpublic%2Fenglish%2Fstandards%2Frelm%2Fgb%2Fdocs%2Fgb277%2Fpdf%2Fd2-abol.pdf&ei=3WLjVNvbBsKXNsPVgZAE&usg=AFQjCNFdqnsO5t_f7vFU1a576byC4AnaMA&sig2=G6r22iG885Ep_63NZ_XnGg&bvm=bv.85970519,d.eXY

[37] Article 3 of Ordonnance-loi No 067/310 du 9 août 1967 portant Code du Travail [Legislative Ordinance No 067/310 of August 9, 1967 on the Labor Code].

[38] Loi No 015-2002 du 16 octobre 2002 Portant Code du Travail [Law 015-2002 of October 16, 2002 on the Labor Code]

[39] Loi No 09/001 du 10 Janvier 2009 portant Protection de l'Enfant [Law 09/001 of January 10, 2009 on the Protection of the Child], http://www.leganet.cd/Legislation/JO/2009/L.09.001.10.01.09.htm

[40] Id., Article 50 of the Law 09/001.Also Article 6(2) of the Loi No 015-2002 du 16 Octobre 2002 portant Code du Travail Congolais [Law 015-2002 of October 2002 on the Congolese Labor Code].

[41] Id., Article 54 of the Law 09/001.

[42] Arrêté Ministériel N° 12/CAB.MIN/TPSI/045 /08 du 08 août 2008 fixant les Conditions de Travail des Enfants en République Démocratique du Congo [Ministerial Order 12/CAB.MIN/TPSI/045/08 of August 8, 2008 on the Working Conditions of Children in the Democratic Republic of Congo].

[43] Id., Article 13.

[44] Ministère du Travail, de l'Emploi, de la Formation Professionnelle et du Dialogue Social, "Protection des Jeunes Travailleurs," (n.d.). http://www.travailler-mieux.gouv.fr/Protection-de-la-sante-des-jeunes.html

[45] Ibid.

[46] The UN Protocol to Prevent, Suppress and Punish Trafficking in Persons, Especially Women and Children of November 15, 2000.

[47] Siddharth Kara, *Sex Trafficking: Inside the Business of Modern Slavery* (New York: Columbia University Press, 2009), 6.

[48] Id., 10.

[49] Ibid.

[50] Dena Hamat and John Tribbett, "A Comparative Analysis of Human Trafficking Legislation and Case Law: Suggestions for Best Practices in Creating Laws Against Human Trafficking," *UNODC Publication*, R76 Project (2009), 8.

[51] Ibid.

[52] Hamat and Tribbett, "A Comparative Analysis" (2009), 8.

[53] Ibid. See also: Liwanga, "Adopting", 19.

[54] "Palermo Protocol," Article 3(c).

[55] Obi Ebbe and Dilip K. Das, *Global Trafficking in Women and Children* (New York: CRC Press, 2008), 8.

[56] Ibid.

[57] "Law 09/001," Article 58.

[58] Ibid.

[59] Samantha Dowling, Karen Moreton, and Leila Wright, "Trafficking for the purposes of labour exploitation: A literature review," *Home Office Online Report* (2007): 8. http://webarchive.nationalarchives.gov.uk/20110218135832/rds.homeoffice.gov.uk/rds/pdfs07/rdsolr1007.pdf

[60] International Labour Organization, "Convention Concerning Forced or Compulsory Labour of 1930," Article 2. http://www.ilo.org/dyn/normlex/en/f?p=NORMLEXPUB:12100:0::NO::P12100_ILO_CODE:C029

[61] UN Gift, "Trafficking for Forced Labour," (2015). http://www.ungift.org/knowledgehub/en/about/trafficking-for-forced-labour.html

[62] United Nations, "The Supplementary Convention on the Abolition of Slavery, the Slave Trade, and Institutions and Practices similar to Slavery of 1956," Article 1(a).

[63] United States Department of State, "Country Narratives: Trafficking in Persons Report 2011: Democratic Republic of Congo." http://www.state.gov/j/tip/rls/tiprpt/2011/164231.htm.

[64] Ibid.

[65] Ravi Srivastava, "Bonded Labour in India: Its Incidence and Pattern," *Cornell University ILR School* (2005): 2. http://digitalcommons.ilr.cornell.edu/forcedlabor/18/.

[66] Ibid.

[67] "Law 09/001," Article 162.

[68] Id., Article 187.

[69] Paul F. A. van Look, Kristian Heggenhougen and Stella R. Quah, *Sexual and Reproductive Health: A Public Health Perspective* (San Diego: Academic Press, 2011), 186. The 2006 combined studies from the World Health Organization and the International Society for Prevention of Child Abuse and Neglect on the reporting of the cases of sexual violence around the world had also concluded that only 20% of women report having been sexually abused as children (See: Paul F. A. van Look, *Sexual and Reproductive Health*, 186). See also: Sara Meger, "Rape of the Congo: Understanding Sexual Violence in the Conflict in the Democratic Republic of Congo," *Journal of Contemporary African Studies* 28 (2010), 130; Stuart Casey-Maslen, *The War Report: Armed Conflict in 2013* (Oxford University Press, 2014), 274.

[70] United States Department of State, "Country Narratives," (2011).

[71] World Bank, Democratic Republic of the Congo. Growth with Governance in the Mining Sector, (2008), 58.

[72] Interviews with NGO workers in Kolwezi. See also: Karen Hayes and Rachel Perks. 2012, "Women in the Artisanal and Small-scale Mining Sector of the Democratic Republic of the Congo" in *High-Value Natural Resources and Peacebuilding* (ed. Paivi Lujala and Siri Aas Rustad, London: Earthscan, 2012), 534.

[73] British Geological Surveys, "Cobalt" (2009).http://www.MineralsUK.com.

[74] Öko-Institut e.V., *Social Impacts of Artisanal Cobalt Mining in Katanga, Democratic Republic of Congo* (2011), 34.

[75] Pact, *Promines* Study: Artisanal Mining in the Democratic Republic of Congo (Washington, DC: Pact, 2010), 47.

[76] Interviews with local NGOs in Lubumbashi and Kolwezi. See also: Öko-Institut e.V., *Social Impacts*, 30.

[77] Gender Action for Peace and Security, *Global Monitoring Checklist on Women, Peace and Security* (2009), 43. See also: Öko-Institut e.V., *Social Impacts*, 30

[78] Loi N° 007/2002 du 11 Juillet 2002 portant Code Minier [Law No 007/2002 of July 11, 2002 relating to the Mining Code].

[79] Article 27 of Law No 007/2002 (Mining Code) stipulates:

"Are not eligible to apply for and obtain mining and/or quarry rights, artisanal miner's cards, trader's cards, as well as the approval as authorized traders for mineral substances from artisanal mining:

a) Government employees and civil servants, magistrates, members of the Armed Forces, the Police and the Security Services, the employees of public entities which are authorized to carry out mining activities. However, this incompatibility does not affect their ability to participate in the capital of mining companies;

b) Any individual who does not have legal capacity under article 215 of the Family Law Code…"

According to the 1987 Family Code, individuals lacking legal capacity include: minors, mentally disabled persons, infirmed persons placed under guardianship, and married women. Therefore, under Article 27(b) of the Mining Code, minors (persons aged less than 18 years) and married women are ineligible to have artisanal miner's cards or trader's card.

[80] Article 26(1) of Mining Code states that "only individuals of age who are Congolese nationals may obtain and hold artisanal miners' cards and traders' cards are eligible to carry out artisanal mining."

[81] Öko-Institut e.V., *Social Impacts of Artisanal*, 34.

[82] Andrew Mollel, "International Adjudication and Resolution of Armed Conflicts in the Africa's Great Lakes: A Focus on the DRC Conflict," *Journal of Law and Conflict Resolution* 10 (2009), 15. See also: Paul T. Zeleza, "Introduction: The Causes & Costs of War in Africa From Liberation Struggles to the 'War on Terror'" in *The Roots of African Conflicts: The Causes and Costs and The Resolution of African Conflicts: The Management of Conflict Resolution and Post-Conflict Reconstruction* 1, 9 (Alfred Nhema and Paul T. Zeleza, eds., 2008); World Without Genocide, *Democratic Republic of Congo*.

http://worldwithoutgenocide.org/genocides-and-conflicts/congo..

[83] Virgil Hawkins, "Stealth Conflicts: Africa's World War in the DRC and International Consciousness," *The Journal of Humanitarian Assistance*. https://sites.tufts.edu/jha/archives/71...

[84] United Nations, *Panel of Experts on the Illegal Exploitation of Natural Resources and other Forms of Wealth of the Democratic Republic of Congo*, (New York: United Nations, 2003).

http://www.un.org/en/sc/repertoire/subsidiary_organs/groups_and_panels.shtml

[85] United States Department of State, *Trafficking in Persons Report* (2015), 127.

[86] Eric Edmonds and Nina Pavcnik, "Child Labor in the Global Economy," *Journal of Economic Perspectives* 19, no 1 (2005): 202.

[87] Hannah Poole Hahn, Karen Hayes, and Azra Kacapor, *Breaking the Chain: Ending the Supply of Child-mined Minerals* (Washington, DC: Pact, 2013), 17.

[88] Ibid.

[89] Ibid.

[90] Hahn, Hayes, and Kacapor, *Breaking the Chain*, 23.

[91] United States Department of State, "Country Narratives," (2011).

[92] Ibid.

[93] "Palermo Protocol," Article 9.

[94] Liwanga, "Adopting," 15.

[95] Ibid.

[96] Loi N° 06/018 du 20 Juillet 2006 modifiant et complétant le Décret du 30 Janvier 1940 portant Code Pénal Congolais [Law 06/018 amending and completing the Decree of January 30, 1940 relating to the Congolese Penal Code].

[97] Id., Article 174(b).

[98] Id., Article 174(c).

[99] Id., Article 174(n).

[100] Id., Article 174(e).

[101] Article of 174(e) Law 06/018 stipulates: "Sex slavery is the fact of exercising the power(s) attached to the ownership of a person, including detaining or imposing a similar deprivation of liberty or buying, selling, lending, trading that person for sexual purposes, and constraint that person to perform one or more sexual acts." Also: Liwanga, "Adopting," 20.

[102] Liwanga, "Adopting," 19.

[103] Loi n° 015-2002 du 16 Octobre 2002 Portant Code du Travail [Law 015-2002 of October 16, 2002 on the Code of Labor].

[104] Id., Article 2.

[105] Id., Article 3.

[106] Ibid. According to the Congolese Labor Code, the worst forms of child labor also comprise acts of child bonded labor.

[107] Liwanga, "Adopting," 16.

[108] Ibid.

[109] "Law 09/001," Article 162.

[110] Id., Article 53(1).

[111] Id., Article 53(2)(a).

[112] Ibid.

[113] Id., Article 53(2)(b).

[114] Articles 23 and 27(b) of the Mining Code.

[115] Id., Article 299.

[116] Id., Article 302.

[117] Liwanga, "Adopting," 16.

CHAPTER 2 - Endnotes

[118] Diane Kayongo-Male and Parveen Walji, *Children at Work in Kenya* (Nairobi: Oxford University Press, 1984), 3–4.

[119] Loretta Bass, *Child Labor in Sub-Saharan Africa* (Colorado: Lynne Rienner Publishers, 2004), 15–16.

[120] Anne Kielland and Maurizia Tovo, *Children at Work: Child Labor Practices in Africa* (Colorado: Lynne Rienner Publishers, 2006), 6.

[121] Ibid.

[122] History World, "The Democratic Republic of Congo: Congo Free State: 1885–1908," http://www.historyworld.net/wrldhis/PlainTextHistories.asp?historyid=ad34

[123] United States Department of State, "Country Narratives: Trafficking in Persons Report 2011: Democratic Republic of Congo," http://www.state.gov/j/tip/rls/tiprpt/2011/164231.htm.

[124] Anne Kielland and Maurizia Tovo, *Children at Work*, 20–21.

[125] Kaushik Basu and Pham Hoang Van, "Economics of Child Labor," *American Economic Review* 88, no.3 (1998): 415.

[126] UNDP, "Multidimensional Poverty Index," *Human Development Index* (2014). http://hdr.undp.org/en/content/table-6-multidimensional-poverty-index-mpi.

[127] Peter Ebigbo et al., *Child Labour in Africa* (Nigeria: African Network for the Prevention and Protection against Child Abuse and Neglect, 1986), 56.

[128] Ibid.

[129] ILO/IPEC-SIMPOC, "Explaining the Demand and Supply Chain of Child Labour: A Review of Underlying Theories" (2007):13. See also: Kielland and Tovo, *Children at Work*, 23; Kara, *Bonded Labor*, 41.

[130] *Henry* Muayila and Eric Tollens, "*Assessing the Impact of Credit Constraints on Farm Household Economic Welfare in the Hinterland of Kinshasa, Democratic Republic of Congo," African Journal of Food, Agriculture, Nutrition and Development 12, no 3 (2012): 6096,*
http://www.ajol.info/index.php/ajfand/article/view/77092/67554

[131] Article 43(5) of the Constitution of the Democratic Republic of Congo of 2006.

[132] Banque Mondiale, *Le Système Educatif de la République Démocratique du Congo: Priorités et Alternatives* (2005), 55.

[133] World Bank, "Data," (2015). http://data.worldbank.org/indicator/SE.XPD.PRIM.PC.ZS

[134] Ibid.

[135] Central Intelligence Agency, "The World Factbook," (2013). https://www.cia.gov/library/publications/the-world-factbook/fields/2127.html

[136] Poole, Hayes, and Kacapor, *Breaking the Chain,* 27.

[137] Ibid.

[138] Ibid.

[139] Gerry Rodgers and Guy Standing, *Child Work, Poverty and Underdevelopment* (Geneva: International Labour Organization, 1981), 23.

[140] Liwanga, "Adopting," 17.

[141] Chi A. Mgbako and Katherine Glenn, "Witchcraft Accusation and Human Rights: Case Studies from Malawi," *Geo. Wash. Int'l L. Rev.* 43 (2011), 389. See also: *International Business Times*, "DR Congo's Witchcraft Epidemic: 50,000 Children Accused of Sorcery," www.ibtimes.co.uk/branded-witch-bbc-democratic-republic-congo-kindoki-469216 (hereafter cited as "IBTimes, 'DR Congo's Witchcraft Epidemic,'").

[142] "Exorcism Punishes Kids for Family's Woes," *The Local,*
http://www.thelocal.se/20130514/47886

[143] Cindi John, "Exorcisms are Part of our Culture," *BBC News*, June 3, 2005.

[144] "Law 09/001," Article 162.

[145] Id., Article 187.

[146] Liwanga, "Adopting," 17.

[147] United States Department of State, "Trafficking in Persons Report 2012: Country Narratives-Democratic Republic of Congo,"
http://www.state.gov/j/tip/rls/tiprpt/2012/192366.htm

[148] Article 7 of the Ordonnance-Loi No 82-020 du 31 Mars 1982 portant Code d'Organisation et Compétence Judiciaire [Ordinance-Law 82-020 of March 31, 1982 on the Code of Organization and Judicial Competence].

[149] African Economic Outlook, *Congo, Democratic Republic*, (2012), 4.

[150] Liwanga, "Economics," 123.

[151] Ibid. See also: "Mining Code," Article 109.

[152] Ibid.

[153] Ibid.

[154] Ibid.

[155] World Bank, *Democratic Republic of Congo Growth*, 56.

[156] Poole, Hayes, and Kacapor, *Breaking the Chain*, 8.

[157] World Bank, *Democratic Republic of Congo Growth*, 56.

[158] Ibid.

[159] Ibid.

[160] Sara Nordband and Petter Bolme, *Powering the Mobile World: Cobalt Production for Batteries in the Democratic Republic of Congo and Zambia*, (2007), 30–32.

[161] Ibid. See also: UNICEF, "In DR Congo, UNICEF supports efforts to help child labourers return to school,"
http://www2.unicef.org:60090/infobycountry/drcongo_62627.html

[162] Susan Gunn, "Combating child labour in Congo," BMS World Mission, (May 27, 2010), http://www.bmsworldmission.org/news-blogs/blogs/combating-child-labour-congo

[163] Kara, *Sex Trafficking*, 33.

[164] Didier Kilondo Nguya, "Ménages Gécamines, Précarité et Economie Populaire" (DEA diss., Université Catholique de Louvain, 2004),

http://www.memoireonline.com/11/07/709/m_menages-gecamines-precarite-economie-populaire35.html

[165] Roger-Claude Liwanga, "Child Miners Face Death for Tech," *CNN Freedom Project*, June 26, 2013.

CHAPTER 3 - Endnotes

[166] Geoview, "Musonoi," (n.d.). http://cd.geoview.info/musonoi,922414

[167] Law No 007/2002 of July 11, 2002 relating to the Congolese Mining Code [Loi No 007/2002 du 11 Juillet 2002 portant Code Minier Congolais], Article 1 (21).

[168] Pact, *Promines Study: Artisanal Mining in the Democratic Republic of Congo* (Washington, DC: Pact, 2010), 48.

http://www.congomines.org/wp-content/uploads/2011/10/PACT-2010-ProminesStudyArtisanalMiningDRC.pdf

[169] Ibid.

[170] Environmental Health Perspectives, "Quicksilver and Gold: Mercury Pollution from Artisanal and Small-Scale Gold Mining," *Environmental Health Perspectives* 120, no. 11, (2012), http://ehp.niehs.nih.gov/120-a424/

[171] *Ibid.*

[172] Ibid.

[173] Pact, *Promines Study,* 49-50.

[174] Ibid.

[175] Ibid.

[176] Ibid.

[177] International Labour Organization, "Convention against the Worst Forms of Child Labour," Article 3(d).

[178] Kielland and Tovo, *Children at Work*, 126.

[179] New Mexico Bureau Geology and Mineral Resources, "What Decision Makers Should Know About Soils in New Mexico," (2001).

https://geoinfo.nmt.edu/geoscience/hazards/collabsible.html

[180] Pact, *Promines Study*, 48.

[181] Philip Graitcer and Leonard Lerer, *Child Labor and Health: Quantifying the Global Health Impacts of Child Labor*, (World Bank, 1998), 12.

[182] Ibid.

[183] Liwanga, "Child Miners Face Death for Tech."

[184] *Human Rights Watch, "Ghana: Mine Accident Highlights Risk to Children," (2013). http://www.hrw.org/news/2013/06/13/ghana-mine-accident-highlights-risk-children*

[185] *Mbazi* is the name of copper ores in the Swahili language.

[186] Poole, Hayes, and Kacapor, *Breaking the Chain*, 19.

[187] Kielland and Tovo, *Children at Work*, 127.

[188] Ibid.

[189] Ibid.

[190] Myriam Elenge, Alain Leveque, and Christophe de Brouwer, "Occupational Accidents in Artisanal Mining in Katanga, DRC," *International Journal of Occupational Medicine and Environmental Health* 26, no.2 (2013): 265–274.

[191] Ibid.

[192] Ibid.

[193] Chris Bird, "The Hard Road to Healthcare for Eastern Congo's Poor," *The Guardian*, (10 April 2012),
http://www.theguardian.com/global-development/poverty-matters/2012/apr/10/hard-road-healthcare-congo-poor

[194] Poole, Hayes, and Kacapor, *Breaking the Chain*, 24.

[195] Ibid.

[196] Pact, *Promines Study*, 96.

[197] Myriam Elenge and Christophe de Brouwer, "Problems of Pathologies related to Toxicological Risks in Small Scale Mining. Case of Katanga Province (D.R.C.): A Review of the Literature," *Journal International de Santé de Travail*, no.1 (2010): 28–39.

[198] Ibid.

[199] Ibid.

[200] Kielland and Tovo, *Children at Work*, 127.

[201] Ibid.

[202] Ibid.

[203] Emmanuel Esguerra, *An Analysis of the Causes and Consequences of Child Labor in the Philippines*, International Labor Organization, (2003), 13.

[204] Work Bank, *Democratic Republic of Congo: Health, Nutrition and Population* (2005), 31.

[205] "The Democratic Republic of Congo," UNAIDS,
http://www.unaids.org/en/regionscountries/countries/democraticrepublicofthecongo/

[206] Poole, Hayes, and Kacapor, *Breaking the Chain*, 24.

[207] Pact, *Promines Study*, 95.

[208] Kielland and Tovo, *Children at Work*, 129.

[209] *Bryan Maybee, Melissa Mungaven, Kseniya Polukhina, and Brandi Bagent,*
"Psychological Impact," Global Child Labor,
https://sites.google.com/site/globalchildlabor/psychological-impact

[210] Martin Woodhead, "Psychosocial Impacts of Child Work: A Framework for Research, Monitoring and Intervention," *International Journal of Children's Rights* 12, no.4 (2004): 321–377.

[211] Ibid.

[212] *Ibid.*

[213] *Maybee et al., "Psychological Impact."*

[214] Sarita Bharti and Shalini Agarwal "Physical and Psychological Hazards Faced by Child Labour--A Review Article" *IOSR Journal Of Humanities And Social Science* 13, no 6 (2013): 29–33.

[215] Ibid. See also: Maybee et al., "Psychological impact."

[216] Ibid.

[217] Yvonne Rafferty, "The Impact of Trafficking on Children: Psychological and Social Policy Perspectives," *Child Development Perspectives* 2, no 1 (2008): 13–18.

[218] Kielland and Tovo, *Children at Work*, 132.

[219] Ibid.

[220] Ibid.

[221] Woodhead, "Psychosocial Impacts of Child Work."

[222] Ibid.

[223] Ibid.

[224] Kielland and Tovo, *Children at Work*, 132.

[225] Ibid.

[226] Poole, Hayes, and Kacapor, *Breaking the Chain*, 23.

[227] Ibid.

[228] Maybee, et al., "Psychological Impact."

[229] Ibid.

[230] Ibid.

[231] Ibid.

[232] Ibid.

[233] Federico Allais and Frank Hagemann, "Child Labour and Education: Evidence from SIMPOC Surveys," Working paper, (Geneva: International Labor Organization, 2008): 2–6.

[234] Ibid.

[235] Ibid.

[236] Ibid.

[237] Ibid.

[238] Ibid.

[239] Gordon Brown, "Child Labour and Educational Disadvantage--Breaking the Link, Building Opportunity," (Office of the UN Special Envoy for Global Education, 2012): 35.

[240] Ibid.

[241] Ibid.

[242] Liwanga, "Economics," 126.

[243] Allais and Hagemann, "Child Labour and Education," 12.

[244] Ibid.

[245] Ibid.

[246] Ibid.

²⁴⁷ Ibid.

²⁴⁸ Ibid.

²⁴⁹ Prince Kyamwami, "Travail des Enfants dans le Site Minier d'Exploitation Artisanale de Bisie en Territoire de Walikale: Une Crise Oubliée en République Démocratique du Congo," Bureau d'Etudes, d'Observation et de Coordination pour le Développement du Territoire de Walikale (2003): 19.

²⁵⁰ Kielland and Tovo, *Children at Work*, 131.

²⁵¹ Id., 141.

²⁵² Liwanga, "Child Miners Face Death for Tech."

²⁵³ Kielland and Tovo, *Children at Work*, 143.

CHAPTER 4 - Endnotes

²⁵⁴ Benita Beamon, "Supply Chain Design and Analysis: Models and Methods," *International Journal of Production Economics* 55, no.3 (1998): 282.

²⁵⁵ Ibid.

²⁵⁶ University of Central Arkansas, "What is a Supply Chain?" (2004). www.sbaer.uca.edu/publications/supply_chain_management/pdf/01.pdf

²⁵⁷ Organization for Economic Cooperation and Development, "The OECD Due Diligence Guidance for Responsible Supply Chains of Minerals from Conflict-Affected and High-Risk Areas: Second Edition," *OECD Publishing* (2013), http://dx.doi.org/1017887/9789264185050-en

²⁵⁸ Ibid.

²⁵⁹ Ibid.

²⁶⁰ Ibid.

²⁶¹ Ibid.

²⁶² World Bank, *Democratic Republic of Congo Growth*, 56.

²⁶³ Article 109 of the Mining Code.

²⁶⁴ Pact, *Promines Study*, 41–42.

²⁶⁵ Ibid.

²⁶⁶ Id., article 1(33).

²⁶⁷ Id., article 117.

²⁶⁸ Id., article 1(10).

²⁶⁹ Id., article 117.

²⁷⁰ Liwanga, "Economics."

²⁷¹ Inter-ministerial Decree No 122/CAB.MINE/MINES/01/2013 and No782/CAB.MIN/FINANCES/2013 on the Regulation of the Export of Retailing Products [Arrêté Interministeriel No 122/CAB.MINE/MINES/01/2013 and No782/CAB.MIN/FINANCES/2013 portant Réglementation des Exportations des Produits Marchands].

²⁷² Emery Mukendi Wafwana, Jonathan van Kempen, and Fulgence Kalema Bwatunda, "L'Interdiction d'Exportation de Concentrés de Cuivre et Cobalt en RDC

Sous Analyse," http://www.lexology.com/library/detail.aspx?g=60d620e7-5275-44ce-98e8-aef48d99e8ee

[273] "La RDC reporte l'embargo sur les exportations de minerais," Jeune Afrique, http://economie.jeuneafrique.com/regions/afrique-subsaharienne/18438-la-rdc-reporte-lembargo-sur-les-exportations-de-minerais.html

[274] Wafwana, Kempen, and Bwatunda, "L'Interdiction d'Exportation."

[275] Jeune Afrique, "La RDC reporte l'embargo."

[276] Cobalt Development Institute, "Cobalt Facts," (n.d.). http://www.thecdi.com/cobaltfacts.php

[277] Ibid.

[278] Ibid.

[279] Ibid.

[280] ECOMIN mining model, "Traceability of minerals," (2011). http://www.ecomin.co/traceable_minerals.html

[281] Ibid.

[282] Dorothea Hilhorst, Disaster, Conflict and Society in Crisis: Everyday Politics of Crisis Response (Abingdon: Routledge Humanitarian Studies, 2013), 136. See also: Section 1502(e)(4) of the Dodd-Frank Wall Street Reform and Consumer Protection Act.

[283] Section 1502(e)(4) of the Dodd-Frank Wall Street Reform and Consumer Protection Act.

[284] See *supra* note 84. http://www.un.org/en/sc/repertoire/subsidiary_organs/groups_and_panels.shtml

[285] Section 1502(e)(4) of the Dodd-Frank Wall Street Reform and Consumer Protection Act.

[286] ECOMIN mining model, "Traceability of minerals."

[287] Ibid.

[288] OECD, "The OECD Due Diligence Guidance."

[289] Liwanga, "Economics," 121.

[290] Ibid.

[291] Ibid.

[292] Steve Quinlivan, "UN Report Indicates Continued Smuggling of Conflict Minerals in DRC Region," *Dodd-Frank*, http://dodd-frank.com/un-report-indicates-continued-smuggling-of-conflict-minerals-in-drc-region/

[293] Cobalt Development Institute, "Cobalt Facts."

[294] See: Table 4.6 Application for Coltan.

[295] Frank Melcher et al, "Fingerprinting of conflict minerals: columbite-tantalite ("coltan") ores," *Society of Geology Applied to Mineral Deposits,* News 23 (2008): 7.

[296] Ibid.

[297] Electronic Industry Citizenship Coalition, "History-EICC," (2015). http://www.eiccoalition.org/about/history/

[298] Philips, "Conflict Minerals," (2014).

http://www.philips.com/about/company/businesses/suppliers/conflict_minerals.page.
See also: Global e-Sustainability Initiative, "Extraction of Metals," (2015).
http://gesi.org/portfolio/project/15

[299] Ibid.

[300] Ibid.

[301] Nicholas Bray, "Minerals Not to Die For," (2012).

http://www.oecdobserver.org/news/fullstory.php/aid/3801/Minerals_not_to_die_for.
html

[302] U.S. Securities and Exchange Commission, "The Investor's Advocate: How the
SEC Protects Investors, Maintains Market Integrity, and Facilitates Capital
Formation," http://www.sec.gov/about/whatwedo.shtml#.VJGQvnvg_-M

[303] Ibid.

[304] Ibid.

[305] Executive Order 13671--Taking Additional Steps to Address the National
Emergency With Respect to the Conflict in the Democratic Republic of the Congo.
Federal Register, Vol.79, no.132, July 10, 2014.

[306] Id., Section (1)(ii)(C)(1).

[307] Id., Section (1)(ii)(C)(7).

[308] Office of Foreign Asset Control, "Democratic Republic of Congo Sanctions
Program," August 13, 2013.

[309] Ibid.

[310] Ibid.

[311] Ibid.

[312] Hogan Lovells, Paul Hilton, and Lillian Tsu, "Private companies now subject to
sanctions for purchasing conflict minerals," *Lexology*. (2014).

http://www.lexology.com/library/detail.aspx?g=b3344acf-b9b7-481f-a0c9-
775e31b48215

[313] 1,321 companies filed reports in 2014, while 1,283 filed reports in 2015. See: US
Government Accountability Office, "Report to Congressional Committees on SEC
Conflict Minerals Rule Department of Labor," (2016): 16.

http://www.gao.gov/assets/680/679232.pdf

[314] In addition to the DRC, there are other countries that are also concerned by the
conflict minerals laws, including: Angola, Burundi, Central African Republic, the
Republic of the Congo, Rwanda, South Sudan, Tanzania, Uganda, and Zambia.

[315] US Government Accountability Office, "Report to Congressional Committees on
SEC Conflict Minerals Rule Department of Labor," (2015): 15.
http://www.gao.gov/assets/680/672051.pdf

[316] Securities and Exchanges Commission, "Rule for Disclosing Use of Conflict
Minerals," August 2012, 17 CFR PARTS 240 and 249b, [Release No. 34-67716;
File No. S7-40-10], RIN 3235-AK84

[317] National Association of Manufacturers vs. Security and Exchange Commission
(District of Columbia Circuit) No. 13-5252 (2014).

[318] US Department of Labor, "Labor Productivity and Costs," (2015). http://www.bls.gov/lpc/

[319] Organization for Economic Cooperation and Development, "Measuring Productivity: Measurement of Aggregate and Industry-Level Productivity Growth," *OECD Publishing* (2001): 11.

[320] Id., 13–14.

[321] Liwanga, "Economics."

[322] Ibid.

[323] Ibid.

[324] Ibid.

[325] Ibid.

[326] Ibid.

[327] Ibid.

[328] Poole, Hayes, and Kacapor, *Breaking the Chain,* 23.

[329] Information collected from interviews with informants in Katanga, DRC.

[330] As of December 2014, the cobalt price at the global market was estimated at $31,600 per ton (1000kg). See: "Cobalt Prices and Cobalt Price Charts," Investment Mines, http://www.infomine.com/investment/metal-prices/cobalt/.

[331] The exportation tax for cobalt and copper ores in the DRC is set up at 1% of the value of the transaction. See: Inter-ministerial Decree N° 3154/CAB.MIN/MINES/01/2007 and N° 031/CAB.MIN/FINANCES/2007 of August 9, 2007 on the Fixing of the Rates of Fees, Taxes and Charges to be Levied on the Initiative of the Minister of Mines [Arrêté interministériel N° 3154/CAB.MIN/MINES/01/2007 et N° 031/CAB.MIN/FINANCES/2007 du 09 août 2007 portant Fixation des Taux des Droits, Taxes et Redevances à Percevoir sur l'Initiative du Ministre des Mines].

CHAPTER 5 - Endnotes

[332] Andrew Mzembe and Yvonne Downs, "Managerial and Stakeholder Perceptions of an Africa-based Multinational Mining Company's Corporate Social Responsibility," *The Extractive Industries and Society* 1 (2014): 225.

[333] Helena Ranängen and Thomas Zobel, "Revisiting the 'How' of Corporate Social Responsibility in Extractive Industries and Forestry," *Journal of Cleaner Production* 84 (2014): 299.

[334] Mzembe and Downs, "Managerial and Stakeholder Perceptions."

[335] World Vision, (2012). "It is a Corporate Responsibility to Address Forced and Child Labour, Not Mine. Discuss."

[336] Mariam Farooq, Omer Farooq, and Sajjad Jasimuddin, "Employees Response to Corporate Social Responsibility: Exploring the Role of Employees' Collectivist Orientation," *European Management Journal* 32 (2014): 917.

[337] World Business Council for Sustainable Development, "Corporate Social Responsibility: Making Good Business Sense," (2000): 3.

[338] European Union, "Corporate Social Responsibility," (2014).
http://ec.europa.eu/enterprise/policies/sustainable-business/corporate-social-responsibility/index_en.htm

[339] Nicole Fallon, "What is Corporate Social Responsibility?," *Business News Daily*, December 22, 2014. http://www.businessnewsdaily.com/4679-corporate-social-responsibility.html

[340] Article 451 of the Decree No 038/2003 of March 26, 2003 on the Mining Regulations [Decret No 038/2003 du 26 Mars 2003 portant Réglement Minier], www.legalnet.cd/Legislation/Droiteconomique/CodeMinier/D.038.2003.26.03.2003.htm

[341] La Plateforme des Organisations de la Société Civile Intervenant dans le Secteur Minier au Katanga (POM), "Propositions d'Amendement du Code Minier," June 2012.

[342] Ibid.

[343] Ibid.

[344] Ibid.

[345] Action Contre l'Impunité pour les Droits de l'Homme, *Les Investissements Privés et Publics Chinois dans le Secteur Minier au Katanga: Bonne Gouvernance et Droit de l'Homme* (2010).

[346] Id., 22.

[347] Ibid.

[348] *BBC News*, "Glencore Linked to Acid Waterfall in DR Congo," April 16, 2012.
http://www.bbc.com/news/business-17726865

[349] John Sweeney, "Mining Giant Glencore Accused in Child Labour and Acid Dumping Row," *The Guardian*, April 14, 2012.
http://www.theguardian.com/business/2012/apr/14/glencore-child-labour-acid-dumping-row

[350] *Facing Finance*, "Glencore: Environmental Damage, Human Rights Violations, Tax Dodging at Katanga," (n.d.).
http://www.facing-finance.org/en/database/cases/katanga-mining/

[351] Johanna Janssson, "CSR Practice in the DRC's Mining Sector by Chinese Firms," *Policy Brief* 9, (2010). See also Mzembe and Downs, "Managerial and Stakeholder Perceptions."

[352] POM, "Propositions d'Amendement du Code Minier."

[353] Ibid.

[354] Emmanuel Raufflet, Luciano Cruz, and Luc Bres, "An Assessment of Corporate Social Responsibility Practices in the Mining and Oil and Gas Industries," *Journal of Cleaner Production* 84 (2014): 256.

[355] Ibid.

[356] Janssson, "CSR Practice in the DRC." See also Mzembe and Downs, "Managerial and Stakeholder Perceptions."

[357] Ibid.

[358] World Vision, "It is a Corporate Responsibility."

[359] Ibid.

[360] Jamie Gordon, "The Economic Implications of Child Labor: A Comprehensive Approach to Labor Policy," Unpublished paper, Duke University (2008): 9.

[361] Ibid. See also: Alan Krueger, "Observations on International Labor Standards and Trade," NBER

Working Paper 5632 (1996).

[362] Ibid.

[363] Ranängen and Zobel, "Revisiting the 'How' of Corporate."

[364] Ibid.

[365] Gordon, "The Economic Implications of Child Labor."

[366] Eric Edmonds and Nina Pavcnik, "Child Labor in the Global Economy," *Journal of Economic Perspectives* 19, no 1 (2005): 213.

[367] Henry *Muayila and Eric Tollens,* "Assessing the Impact of Credit Constraints on Farm Household Economic Welfare in the Hinterland of Kinshasa, Democratic Republic of Congo," African Journal of Food, Agriculture, Nutrition and Development 12, no 3 (2012).

http://www.ajol.info/index.php/ajfand/article/view/77092/67554

[368] Gordon, "The Economic Implications of Child Labor."

[369] Ibid.

[370] Ranängen and Zobel, "Revisiting the 'How' of Corporate."

[371] Raufflet, Cruz, and Bres, "An Assessment of Corporate Social."

[372] World vision, "It is a Corporate Responsibility."

APPENDIX E - Endnotes

[373] Securities and Exchanges Commission, "Rule for Disclosing Use of Conflict Minerals," August 2012, 17 CFR PARTS 240 and 249b, [Release No. 34-67716; File No. S7-40-10], RIN 3235-AK84

[374] Ibid.

[375] Ibid.

[376] Ibid.

[377] National Association of Manufacturers vs. Security and Exchange Commission (District of Columbia Circuit) No. 13-5252 (2014).

[378] Id., 10.

[379] Id.,8.

[380] Id., 10.

[381] Id., 8-9.

[382] Id., 10.

[383] Id., 23.

[384] Ibid.

www.ingramcontent.com/pod-product-compliance
Lightning Source LLC
Chambersburg PA
CBHW072234290326
41934CB00008BA/1288